(W)hole

My Journey to W

By Amber Washington

ISBN: 9798296930873

Printed in the United States of America

Cover design by Gisele Chastain

Author website: www.wholeheals.com

Author's Note

Every memory in this book comes from my lived experience. Where possible, I've supported events with official records, written reports, or documents in my possession. This story is mine, and I've done my best to tell it with truth, integrity, and care.

Some names have been changed. Some moments may seem unbelievable, because sometimes what really happened doesn't fit neatly into words.

I know my truth. And I stand by it.

Trigger Warning

This memoir contains themes of sexual abuse, trauma, and emotional distress. While written with care and intention, it may bring up strong emotions. Please read with compassion for yourself. Pause when needed. Return when you're ready. You are not alone.

They don't disbelieve you—they just find it easier not to believe you. Because belief demands accountability.

Legal Disclaimer

This memoir is not a substitute for professional therapy, diagnosis, or medical care. If you are experiencing emotional distress or trauma-related symptoms, please seek support from a qualified mental health professional.

Dedication

This book is for me.

For little Amber, who carried far too much.

For teenage Amber, who bore the weight of shame and self-hatred she didn't deserve.

For adult Amber, who spent years searching for her place in a world that never felt like it was made for her.

And for the Amber I am today—grateful for every version of me who survived long enough to tell this story.

Chin up. Face forward. Voice steady. We made it. And we are just getting started!

To my sons.

You are my why. My light. My heartbeat.

You survived the worst of me and somehow became the best of me.

You have become the protectors I searched for my entire life. My heroes.

Thank you for standing by me in my becoming. For showing me what unconditional love looks like.

You are the proof that love outlives pain. That healing is possible, that cycles can break.

This story may begin in the darkness, but it ends in you.

Acknowledgments

To Heather—my ride-or-die. We've cried more tears than two humans should be allowed. We love without keeping score. You've been my constant, my safe, my forever.

To my Mom—for your love, your growth, and your courage to face hard truths.

To my best girlfriends—weekends dancing, good food, road trips, and laughing till we can't breathe. You love all of me, and all of me loves you. JAM forever!

To my community—thank you for making healing possible in a place that once felt like hell.

To my friends—you know who you are—thank you for showing up, holding space, and reminding me who I am.

To my therapists, Dok and Marilyn—for walking me through the dark with wisdom, compassion, and belief in my healing.

To David—for hiring me into tech when I didn't yet believe I belonged. For seeing something in me before I could see it in myself. Your belief changed the course of my life.

To Melissa Di Donato and April Moh—for opening the door to sharing my story and helping me realize that vulnerability and leadership can—and should—coexist.

To SUSE—for being more than just a workplace. Thank you to everyone there who has been part of this journey—past or present.

To every survivor—whether you're finding your voice, reclaiming your power, or still trying to breathe through the weight of it all—this is for you. You are not alone.

To Saprea—for being a lighthouse for survivors around the world, guiding us with compassion, purpose, and unwavering dedication.

And to my Saprea sisters—you are sacred to me. Though our stories are uniquely our own, our strength is shared. You've reminded me that healing is never solitary—it's stitched together in the spaces between us.

To everyone who played a role in my story—you shaped me.
To those who lifted me—I'm grateful.
To those who wounded me—this book doesn't thank you. It outgrows you.

Foreword

By Susanne Lay

I first saw Amber's strength before I had the language to understand it. She was only two and a half when she looked me in the eye—defiant, red-faced, and determined—and said, "No." At the time, I saw disobedience. What I know now is that I was witnessing her spirit—the same spirit that would one day help her survive the unthinkable.

As a young mother, I defaulted to what I'd been taught: discipline through control, silence, and consequence. It didn't take long for me to realize that this pattern wasn't just ineffective—it was harmful. I began to shift. Slowly. Painfully. I prayed for patience. I started to unlearn the generational responses I had inherited. And in that process, I began to see Amber differently—not as a rebellious child, but as a fiercely strong one. One who would need every ounce of that strength for the road ahead.

When Amber disclosed her abuse in 1989, I didn't know how to hold it. I stayed busy. I buried it. I wrote almost nothing in my journal—not about the conversation, not about confronting her abuser, and not about the emotional wreckage we were all navigating. I see now how my silence mirrored the world's. And how, despite my best intentions, Amber was left to carry the weight alone. I hoped she would "get over it." I wanted her to be okay. But I didn't know how to walk with her through it. And for that, I hold deep remorse.

Over the years, I've watched my daughter do what so many survivors are told not to: speak up. Ask hard questions. Refuse to perform healing for anyone else's comfort. Her story is not just one of trauma—it's one of tenacity, truth, and transformation.

Writing this foreword is part of my own healing. I've had to face how silence protects harm. How busyness can mask denial. And how the best way to love someone in their pain is not to fix it, but to see it—and to stay.

To anyone reading this: don't be silenced. Use your voice. Healing is possible—but only if we tell the truth, to ourselves and each other. Amber's story is a light. It's uncomfortable, raw, and unflinchingly honest. It's also a roadmap—for what happens when someone refuses to stay buried, and fights to become whole.

With love,
Susanne

Contents

PROLOGUE

Tthe command sliced through the chaos, sharp and final.
"Turn around and put your hands behind your back."

Disbelief. A cold wave washed over me, stealing my breath.
This isn't real. This can't be happening. My mind scrambled—a
frantic mess of jumbled thoughts and raw panic—desperately
searching for an escape hatch from a reality I couldn't comprehend.

My eyes found them—my boys. Tears streamed down their
small faces, their expressions twisted in fear. They were being ushered
away, pulled back into the house, the distance between us stretching
into an impossible, heart-shredding void.

Time warped, slowed—each second an eternity marking their
retreat and my helplessness.

The cold steel clicked around my wrists. My rights were read, a
meaningless drone against the pounding in my ears. *Arrested? Me?
How?*

Anger surged—hot, bitter, blinding.

A push, yes. A moment where simmering rage, fueled by months of manipulation, withheld visits, and blatant disrespect, finally boiled over. But this? Handcuffs? A ride not to the local station, but to the county jail?

The injustice burned—a searing brand on my soul. Others had inflicted so much pain—abuse, lies, betrayal, violence—yet walked free. The universe felt tilted, its scales of justice mocking me.

I was numb, replaying the scene: the shouts, the fear, the shove that sent me sprawling onto unforgiving concrete. I shouldn't have stopped. I shouldn't have been there—not then, not like that. Every nerve screamed it. But the sight of him, preparing to leave when my children should have been with me, detonated something deep inside.

This was the culmination.
Rock bottom.

The day my life imploded—plunging me into the deepest, darkest hole imaginable, leaving behind wreckage I wasn't sure I could ever climb out of.

I wasn't a violent person. I wasn't the monster they painted me to be. But here I was—marked, judged, and carted away like a criminal from the bottom of that abyss.

The weight of the handcuffs felt heavier than just metal; it was the weight of every misstep, every moment of lost control, every injustice I had endured leading up to this catastrophic point.

This was the day I hit the floor of the hole I'd been digging for years.

To understand how the pieces shattered so completely—how a mother fighting for her children ended up buried so deep—you have to go back.

Back to the beginning.

Introduction

(A)mber

On a crisp fall morning, early in November 1980, Amber Dawn was born. With a head full of thick black hair, I was their first child—the bundle of joy they'd anxiously awaited.

In those early days—maybe even years—I was my dad's pride and joy. Or so it felt. I remember the sharp, distinct smell of oil and metal that clung to the air in our garage, a scent forever linked to the image of me—small and eager—standing beside him, handing him wrenches and rags as he tinkered with the gleaming chrome and dark metal of his motorcycle. I felt important then. Involved in his world.

The real thrill, though, was the ride. He'd lift me, squealing, onto the seat in front of him, my small hands gripping the handlebars, the powerful vibration of the engine thrumming through my body before we even moved. Then the roar as we took off, the wind whipping my hair back, the world blurring past in streaks of color.

There's a picture somewhere, capturing that pure joy—me, perched happily on the bike at age two, my grin wide, feeling utterly fearless and adored.

Our home was unique—a small house standing almost alone on nearly half an acre in the middle of a dusty field. It sat just at the edge of an established neighborhood, close enough to belong to the local church ward, but separate enough to feel like our own little world.

It was a lively, sometimes chaotic place. Mom babysat several neighborhood kids to make ends meet, so the house constantly hummed with the energy of small children—laughter, cries, the patter of little feet on linoleum. The screen door seemed to perpetually slam as friends, family, and neighbor kids came and went. Connection felt constant.

Outside, our patch of land was a mini-farmyard, populated by curious goats who'd nibble fingers offered through the fence, clucking chickens scratching in the dirt, and soft-furred rabbits twitching their noses in wooden hutches.

I remember sunny afternoons spent outside during family gatherings. My dad and uncles would spread out a sturdy old blanket, each grabbing a corner. We kids would take turns in the middle, shrieking with terror and delight as they hoisted us up, up, up— launching us toward the vast blue sky before catching us safely again in the sagging center. In those moments, flying weightless for a second, surrounded by the sounds of family and the warmth of the Utah sun, life felt like pure, unadulterated magic.

But even amidst that happy bustle, my own strong-willed personality was making itself known. By the time I was two, my burgeoning independence had become a constant test of my mother's patience. She had only recently given birth to my sister, adding another layer of demand to her already stretched resources. Running on fumes, Mom's patience wore thinner than the worn patches on our sofa. She'd tell me later about the hours she spent trying to manage my stubborn defiance.

I recall one instance vividly: I had strep throat—a common childhood ailment for me—but the pink antibiotic suspension the doctor prescribed tasted like chalky bubblegum gone horribly wrong. Every dose was a battle. Mom would approach with the little plastic measuring spoon, her expression pleading, but I'd clamp my jaw shut, turning my head away with fierce determination. No amount of coaxing ("It will make you feel better!"), hiding it in juice, or gentle threats worked. I simply would not swallow that pink goo.

It was a small, sticky battle—insignificant in the grand scheme of health—but it represented something deeper: the core of resistance within me. An innate refusal to yield, even when it was seemingly for my own good.

Then one night, slumped in a chair after a particularly trying day—exhausted from chasing toddlers and fighting the medicine battle—Mom was struck with a profound awareness. A mother's intuition, perhaps. Maybe, just maybe, I was going to need that stubbornness. Maybe that fiery defiance wasn't just a phase to be extinguished, but a core part of the person I was meant to become. A strength I would desperately need later in life when faced with battles far greater than a spoonful of unwanted medicine.

From that point forward, something shifted in her approach. She still set boundaries, still taught right from wrong—but she worked to nurture that spirit more and fight against it less. She began to see the potential strength hidden within the difficult toddler behavior, the resilience simmering beneath the resistance.

Aside from that powerful motherly instinct, she couldn't possibly know just how much that defiance would, indeed, be needed.

CHAPTER 1

My stomach felt weird—tight and fluttery in a way that wasn't excitement, but dread.

I pressed my face closer to the cool plastic slats of the accordion closet door in my best friend Jackie's bedroom, peering through the narrow gap. The air inside was thick, stale, reeking of worn socks and the faint, sour tang of dirty underwear piled in a hamper somewhere in the shadows. Dust motes danced in the slivers of light filtering through the slats.

I wanted to squeeze my eyes shut, make the images disappear, block out the muffled sounds from the room beyond. I wanted to fling the flimsy door open and run—burst out of the cramped darkness, out of the house, and never look back.

But I was frozen, rooted to the spot, held captive by a sickening knot of fear and a morbid curiosity I didn't understand.

I knew I wasn't supposed to watch. He didn't want me to see what he was doing to her on the bed just feet away. It was part of his twisted game. He did the same thing to Jackie when it was my turn—when she was the one crammed into this suffocating space, forced into the role of silent, helpless witness while I endured his touch.

We were trapped in his cycle, taking turns as victim and unwilling observer, the shared secret hanging heavy and unspoken between us even when we were alone.

How could something feel so wrong, yet be happening? Why didn't he stop? Why didn't we scream? The questions echoed silently in the small, dark space.

Suddenly, the distinct sound of the front door opening upstairs drifted down, followed by footsteps.

He scrambled off the bed, his movements frantic now, pulling up his pants with fumbling haste.
"Get dressed," he hissed at Jackie, his voice low and urgent.

He yanked the closet door open, pulling me out into the relative brightness of the bedroom—just as their mom appeared in the doorway.

Her face was set in its usual disapproving scowl, a look that always seemed directed at me, intensifying the baseline fear I felt whenever she was near. She radiated a perpetual tension—a brittle grumpiness that made my small body instinctively tense up.

Today was no different.

Her sharp eyes swept the room, lingering on Jim's flushed face, Jackie's hastily adjusted clothes, and my own wide-eyed presence near the closet.

"What is going on here?" she huffed, her voice laced with suspicion.

"We were just playing hide and seek, Mom," Jim lied smoothly, the falsehood rolling easily off his tongue, betraying none of the frantic energy from moments before.

His mom looked from him to us, her frown deepening—but she didn't press further.

Maybe she didn't want to know.
Maybe she was too tired.
Or maybe she believed him.

The moment passed. The immediate danger averted—leaving only the residue of fear and the sticky shame of the secret we carried.

This wasn't the first time he had done this—subjected us to his perverse games under the guise of babysitting. Jim was older than us and often left in charge while his parents worked or ran errands.

Jackie was a year older than me, and our lives had been tightly intertwined since we were toddlers—ever since my mom started babysitting them both.

Our shared history was woven with the bright threads of normal childhood:
Building lopsided snowmen in the deep drifts of Utah winters until our fingers were numb and red...
Catching fat, lazy snowflakes on our tongues...
Feeling the exhilarating spray of lake water on hot summer days spent water skiing with her family...
Inventing elaborate games in the vast, sun-baked fields surrounding my home.

We were immersed in the potent magic of childhood innocence then—soaking up the world with wide-eyed wonder, unaware of how fragile it truly was.

An innocence that Jim, with his secret touches and hidden games, was destroying for both of us.

The memory of those carefree days felt distant now, overshadowed by the suffocating secret held within the stale air of Jackie's bedroom closet. And soon after this incident, the fragile boundary between his abuse and my own damaged understanding would crumble completely.

CHAPTER 2

(C)onsequences

That innocence took another, more complicated hit not long after the closet incident. My mom, in addition to watching Jim and Jackie sometimes, also babysat other children from the neighborhood— younger ones. Our house often felt like a bustling daycare center.

One afternoon, she discovered me in the small, detached playhouse in our backyard with one of the little boys she cared for, maybe three or four years old. The playhouse wasn't just any structure; it had been a special Christmas gift from my parents to me and my two sisters. Dad had built it from scratch, pouring his love and effort into its tiny walls and roof. Mom had even made charming little curtains for its windows. They had spent hours creating what they imagined would be a safe, magical play place just for us. That day it was far from a sanctuary.

"Amber! What in the world are you doing?!"

Her voice cracked like a whip from the playhouse doorway, sharp and laced with a horror I'd never heard from her before. The sheer force of it—the raw shock and anger—told me instantly that I was in a kind of trouble I hadn't known existed. Shame flooded me, hot and overwhelming, a physical sensation that started in my stomach and rose to my cheeks. I instinctively hid my eyes, trying to shrink away as tears started to well, stinging and blurring my vision of the scattered plastic tea set on the dusty floor. My small body trembled.

"I'm... I'm... I'm sorry, Mom!" I stammered, the words catching in my throat, thick with unshed tears.

"Get inside! NOW!" she yelled, her anger palpable in a way I'd rarely witnessed. I scrambled out of the playhouse, tripping over my own feet in my haste, and hurried toward the front door of our house, desperate to escape her fury, the little boy's confused whimper echoing behind me.

Inside the cool dimness of the house, seeking a sliver of normalcy—some small comfort—I automatically went to the kitchen and opened the green freezer door, reaching for a popsicle. The familiar cold plastic wrapper felt grounding in my hand, a tiny anchor in the storm of my fear.

Then she came through the door right behind me. My mom, usually so patient, so timid—the one whose footsteps were normally light and barely audible on the linoleum—now entered with heavy steps that echoed unnervingly in the suddenly silent kitchen. Her presence filled the room not with its usual gentle warmth, but with an unbearable, crackling tension.

My cheeks felt like they were on fire. I could barely lift my face to meet her gaze as the flurry of questions began, each one landing like a blow. *She's going to ask. What should I say? Don't tell, don't tell, he said don't tell.*

"Where did you learn that?" she demanded, her voice sharp, unforgiving.

I quickly shoved the cold popsicle into my mouth, biting down hard, the icy sweetness a stark contrast to the burning shame. It was a flimsy shield. I looked away—anywhere but at her piercing blue eyes.

"Amber, where did you learn to do that? Tell me, now!" Her voice rose, insistent, demanding an answer I didn't want to give.

The truth tumbled out in a rush, choked with fear and shame and the cold popsicle melting in my mouth.
"Jim does it to me and Jackie, Mom! I'm sorry! I'm so sorry!"

The events that followed are hazy, fragmented—like trying to recall a dream moments after waking. I vaguely recall going over to Jackie and Jim's house after that, a confusing, awful meeting where my mom, her face grim and pale, confronted their parents with what I'd told her.

I remember the feeling of the stiff couch cushions beneath me in their stale living room, the way Jim's dad wouldn't look directly at me—just stared at a spot on the wall above my head, his jaw tight and pulsing. The air felt thick with unspoken adult horror and disbelief, and I felt so small, so exposed.

It's fuzzy, like watching a movie through thick fog, but the result was stark and immediate: a short time later, their family moved away.

Just like that, they were gone. Jackie—my best friend, the other keeper of our shared, terrible secret—vanished from my life.

I never saw her again. There was no goodbye, no explanation, just an empty house down the street and a gaping hole where our friendship used to be. Losing her felt like losing my only ally—the only other person who truly knew.

Her absence amplified my isolation, leaving me alone with the secret and a gnawing fear that maybe, just maybe, it was all my fault. *Did she blame me for telling?* I had no way of knowing.

Looking back, the signs that something was deeply wrong had been there even before I got caught in the playhouse. My mom confessed later she'd suspected something was amiss for a while.

I'd been drawing strange, unsettling pictures of myself—little figures clad in provocative miniskirts and midriff-baring tops, clothing I didn't own and wouldn't have even known how to imagine without some external, corrupting influence.

My behavior had shifted, too, becoming erratic and unpredictable. I was acting out, inexplicably mean and volatile toward my younger sisters and the other kids Mom watched.

A particularly vivid example of this defiance occurred on my baby brother's blessing day. After church, where Grandma, Grandpa, and even my great-grandparents had been present, we all went home for a nice dinner and to take family pictures.

As soon as we got home, I changed out of my uncomfortable church dress and into my play clothes. My parents immediately yelled at me, telling me to put my dress back on for the pictures. I refused. All the grandparents looked appalled at my defiance, and a wave of embarrassment washed over me, but still, I stubbornly held my ground.

Mom, somehow, eventually convinced me to be in the pictures, but I remained in my comfy clothes—a small, defiant figure amidst a sea of Sunday best.

It was a confusing mix of anger, sadness, and a deep-seated unease I couldn't articulate—all manifesting as stubborn opposition.

When I finally confessed about Jim, prompted by my own disturbing actions in the playhouse, it seemed like the missing piece— the explanation for everything. It was easy for everyone to conclude that this—Jim's abuse—was the sole reason for the drawings, the anger, the shift in my personality.

And while Jim's abuse certainly scarred me, violated my innocence, and contributed significantly to my troubled behavior, the truth was far more complicated—layered with a deeper, more insidious darkness.

It wasn't the only betrayal I was enduring. It wasn't the only secret I was forced to keep. It wasn't even the worst thing happening to me.

CHAPTER 3

(B)efore

Childhood memories can be slippery things—sharp at the edges, hazy in the middle. Looking back now feels like piecing together a shattered mirror: the reflections are there, but fractured, distorted by what came later. Before the cracks appeared—before darkness seeped in at the edges—life felt magical. Truly, breathtakingly magical. Through my young, naïve eyes, the world was perfect, like heaven on earth.

Our extended family formed the vibrant center of that universe, a tight constellation of aunts, uncles, cousins, and grandparents orbiting Grandma and Grandpa's house. Their home stood just one lot away from my great-grandparents', creating a cozy pocket where family felt impossibly close. The house itself was a solid two-story of brown brick, the kind that looked built to last forever. Its yard became the backdrop for countless hours of play.

I remember the Utah sun warm on my back as I knelt beside the big brick planter out front, picking sun-ripened strawberries. Juice stained my fingers; half the berries never made it to Grandma's bowl. The front yard, enclosed by a low half-brick wall perfect for balancing on, held a winding path we turned into a racetrack for tag and cops-and-robbers. Out back, a covered patio offered cool shade and a sturdy, shed-turned-playhouse that smelled of old wood and forgotten tools. A tall slatted fence, hidden behind leafy shrubs, made the yard feel like our own secret world.

Inside, you entered on the top floor, stepping directly into the living room where most of the chaos unfolded. It always carried a faint mix of Grandma's potpourri and something good simmering in the kitchen. Off to the right sat the formal study—Grandma's domain—dominated by her polished piano and generally off-limits to kids. Beyond the living room was the kitchen, the true heart of the home: yeasty bread, savory roasts, holiday gingerbread, pumpkin pie. Down the hall were Grandma's bedroom, a main bath counter lined with Mary Kay pink bottles and powdery perfume, and a guest room where I got to sleep beneath a handmade quilt whenever I was lucky enough to stay overnight.

Downstairs felt like a separate universe—darker, off-limits, a little mysterious. Grandpa slept there (his epic snoring was the official reason). A second living room, paneled and slightly smoky-smelling, felt adult and forbidden. A large storage room brimmed with forgotten boxes. We only descended the creaky stairs when Grandma sent us for something specific—then dashed back up into the light.

Even now, that basement surfaces in my dreams, never overtly terrifying but saturated with unease. I always remembered that basement. But it wasn't until a conversation with my mom recently that I remembered why.

My grandmother had once told me that she suspected something was wrong. But what I hadn't remembered until now was what made her suspect it. She told me her visiting teachers came by one day while I was there, and she asked me to go down to the basement. She said something in the way I responded—my face, my energy, my hesitation—made her pause. She still sent me anyway. And she's carried guilt for that ever since.

When that memory surfaced during the conversation with my mom, I felt it in my body first. My stomach churned. My hands shook. My whole body buzzed like it was holding onto electricity. I thought I might pass out. Even when I talked about it later in therapy, the same wave hit me again. *Something happened in that basement. Maybe more than once.* And even if my memory had buried it, my body hadn't forgotten.

But memory is tricky like that—layered, fragmented, nonlinear. Just as one part of me was holding shadows in that basement, another part was outside in the sun.

Beyond the basement, life carried on—bright, loud, and deceptively normal. Birthdays spilled onto the patio for summer BBQs. I can still smell charcoal lighter fluid, sizzling burgers, and freshly cut grass. There was always shimmering Jell-O salad and someone's famous potato salad in a chipped ceramic bowl. We kids chased each other, sticky with watermelon juice. Grandpa would warn, eyes twinkling, that swallowed seeds would sprout watermelon babies in our bellies—a silly threat that made us giggle and spit seeds for distance.

Christmas was the pinnacle. Grandma and Grandpa's house transformed into a storybook wonderland. A fragrant pine nearly brushed the ceiling; its branches blazed with large colored bulbs and heirloom ornaments. Tinsel dripped like silver icicles. Nearby, an animated Santa figure periodically chuckled, his plush belly shaking as he ho-ho-hoed, sending us into fits of laughter. The whole house glowed with pine, sugar, and anticipation.

Evenings before the big day, we'd huddle on the couch or sprawl on thick carpet under crocheted blankets smelling faintly of cedar. We watched *Rudolph*, *Frosty*, maybe *Babes in Toyland*. The TV's glow, the warmth of piled-on family, my head resting on Mom's lap as she stroked my hair—all of it fused into pure, incandescent safety. Surrounded by people sworn to protect me, life felt whole, unshakable.

I couldn't imagine anything breaking that spell—or that the "off-limits" parts of the house held more than a snoring grandpa or dusty storage.

CHAPTER 4

(S)hadows

But even within that seemingly perfect world of warm Christmases and boisterous family BBQs, shadows were beginning to gather—unnoticed by my innocent eyes. Pinpointing the exact moment the darkness began its insidious creep is impossible, like trying to isolate the first drop of rain before a storm. Looking back, however, the grooming—the careful, patient groundwork for the abuse that would follow—started long before I understood its sinister shape.

I think I was around seven when the explicit abuse began, but the preparation had already begun—silently and deliberately woven into those seemingly happy days.

It started with feeling special. Noticed. Singled out by him—my grandfather.

He had a way of pulling me close under the guise of affection, drawing me onto his lap with casual familiarity. His lap felt bony beneath me, the rough texture of denim scratching against my legs. The heavy musk of his cologne clung to my clothes long after he let me go. "That's my special girl," he'd say, his hand resting just a little too long on my back or leg, his tone warm but secretive, like we were in on something together.

To a little girl who wanted so desperately to be good, to be seen and loved, it felt like love. It felt like being chosen. But deep down, even then, something squirmed. It didn't feel like my mom's hugs or Grandma's kisses on the cheek. It was a different kind of attention— one that felt warm and confusing and, at times, wrong. And yet, how could it be bad if it came from someone who was supposed to love me?

He took me on a trip once—just the two of us—to visit cousins in California. At the time, it felt like a grand adventure. I had no reason not to trust him. We sang silly songs in the car, played guessing games, and he bought me treats at gas stations. I felt proud to be the one grandkid chosen for this trip.

But on the way back, I got hungry, and instead of stopping for food, he pulled out something he had packed: a sandwich made with bologna and peanut butter.

Even as a kid, I knew it was wrong. Not just weird—but wrong. I remember taking one bite, confused by the clash of textures and tastes, and wondering why he would feed me something so disgusting. Later, I asked if we could stop at McDonald's. He said no at first—like it was a punishment, like I was being ungrateful. Hours later, he finally gave in. But by then, I felt too uneasy to eat much. It wasn't just about the sandwich—it was the tone, the control, the strangeness of being alone with someone who was beginning to feel... unpredictable.

Not all the memories from that time feel bad. That's part of what makes it so hard to hold. Some are still soft around the edges, glowing with the kind of innocence I wish had lasted longer.

One of those is Easter. Dying Easter eggs at Grandma's house was one of our favorite traditions. She'd cover the table in newspaper and set out bowls of bright vinegar dye—yellow, pink, blue, green—alongside crayons, stickers, and those little copper wire holders that never quite worked the way we hoped. He was there too, joining in with the grandkids.

I remember sitting next to him, focused on drawing swirls with a white crayon before lowering my egg into the deep blue. He laughed when someone knocked over a bowl, shaking his head with mock exasperation. For that hour, in that warm kitchen with the vinegar sting in the air and everyone's hands stained with color, he just seemed like Grandpa. Safe. Normal. Fun.

That's what makes the betrayal so impossible to digest.

How could the same man who helped me make marbled purple eggs also lead me down into a basement filled with fear? How could he laugh with me one day and manipulate me the next?

That Easter memory—so vivid, so normal—isn't erased by what happened later. It just sits beside it. Like two parallel tracks of truth. One where I felt joy, and one where I felt afraid. The problem is, as time went on, the joyful track began to twist, warped by the weight of what I'd come to understand. Those innocent moments weren't always innocent. And the love I thought I felt wasn't love—it was a lure.

He was laying the groundwork. Each "special" moment was a brick in a carefully built trap. Each compliment a thread in a net I didn't know I was caught in.

This is the impossible duality of grooming: the predator doesn't just steal your safety—they distort your memories. They turn your joy into confusion. Your laughter into shame. Your trust into a weapon used against you.

For those first few years of life, I thought I was living the dream.

I was the apple of his eye.
He was my third word.
I was footloose and fancy free.
He was addicted to pornography.
I was trusting.
He was deceitful.
I was innocent.
He was grooming.
I was his victim.
He was my predator.

The monster under my bed, come to life. My worst nightmare.

CHAPTER 5

(C)onfirmation

T he monster wasn't just under my bed; he was an active, terrifying presence in my life as I turned eight years old. That hidden nightmare—the ongoing reality of his grooming and abuse—became the poisoned lens through which I viewed everything, especially the milestones meant to signify purity and connection within my family's faith.

Reaching the age deemed ripe for eternal covenants felt less like a spiritual awakening and more like a confusing, painful paradox. *How could I be worthy of God's love when I felt so dirty? So trapped in secrets I couldn't speak?*

The constant dissonance between the "special" attention Grandpa gave me and the wrongness I felt deep inside created a desperate yearning for rescue. The Church promised divine comfort—a guiding Holy Ghost who would protect me, maybe even from him. So, as baptism day dawned, I carried not just the typical nerves of a child facing a solemn ceremony, but the heavy, invisible weight of ongoing trauma and the frantic, unspoken hope that maybe—just maybe—this sacred ritual could build a shield. That it could wash away the darkness already consuming me.

It was finally the day.

Baptism day.

I was eight years old—the "age of accountability," according to The Church of Jesus Christ of Latter-Day Saints. My entire family was there, crammed onto the benches alongside friends and familiar faces from our ward. A few other kids nervously awaited their turn, dressed in identical white jumpsuits. We had all been waiting for this milestone. Eight felt significant. Grown-up.

My dad, also dressed in white, stood waiting for me in the waist-deep water of the font. The air was cool and slightly humid, carrying that faint, clean scent unique to still water kept indoors. Ripples shimmered across the pale blue tiles, the surface smooth against my skin, almost silky, but with a chill that made me want to move quickly—yet not too quickly.

The font sat tucked into its own little alcove, a mirror slanted above so the congregation could watch. Every sound seemed amplified in that tiled space—the faint slosh of water against the walls, the shuffle of bare feet on the steps, the low murmur of voices just outside. Two witnesses stood at the edge, their eyes locked on the surface to be sure every inch of me would go under.

I knew the rule. And maybe that's why, as my dad prepared to say the prayer and perform the ordinance, a mischievous thought flickered through my mind: If you make your foot come up and out of the water, he'll have to do it again.

The idea of prolonging the watery part—maybe getting a small laugh—felt appealing. A tiny act of control in a world where I felt increasingly powerless. The baptism itself, the dunking under the water, felt like the fun part.

But it was the confirmation, the ceremony that followed, that I was truly looking forward to. I had pinned my fragile hopes upon it. I had been told—promised even—that this was when I would receive the Holy Ghost. A constant companion. A spiritual guide who would offer comfort, peace, and—most importantly to my anxious heart—alert me when something was wrong. Protect me from danger.

I craved that comfort more than anything.

Back in my Sunday dress, I sat stiffly on a metal chair, my damp hair clinging to my neck. A circle of men from our ward—familiar faces, family friends, priesthood holders deemed "worthy" to administer blessings—gathered around me. Their hands, nearly a dozen in total, settled on my small head.

I remember feeling anxiously excited to receive the Holy Ghost. Hopeful that something sacred would fill me. But one hand felt heavier than the rest—larger, more insistent. I was almost certain it was my grandfather's.

In my memory, it presses down like a warning. Like a reminder to keep our secret.

I closed my eyes tightly, folded my arms just as I'd been taught, and braced myself—for what, I still don't fully know.

"Amber Dawn Lay," I heard my dad's familiar voice begin, solemn and formal, "having been commissioned by Jesus Christ, I lay my hands upon your head and confirm you a member of The Church of Jesus Christ of Latter-Day Saints and say unto you, receive the Holy Ghost."

Okay, I'm ready, I thought, holding my breath, waiting for the overwhelming peace, the undeniable comfort, the whisper of divine presence I'd heard others describe. *Please... let me feel it.*

Nothing.

Just... emptiness.

Silence.

The weight of their hands felt crushing. My body started to shake—an uncontrollable tremor born of disappointment and rising panic. It felt as if the room was closing in on me, the air too thick to breathe.

In my mind's eye, I saw distorted images—everyone looking at me, their faces shifting between disappointment and faint, knowing half-grins. *He knew. God knew. They all knew.*

The realization hit me with the force of a physical blow.

I wasn't worthy.

The abuse, the secrets I carried, the darkness clinging to me—it made me unclean. Unacceptable.

God hadn't answered my desperate prayers for protection from Grandpa. Hadn't intervened when I begged for someone to discover the abuse and make it stop. And now... He was denying me His spirit. His comfort. His love.

It felt final.

He hated me.

The weight of His perceived judgment bore down on my small frame like a punishment I couldn't escape. And in that moment—surrounded by hands meant to bless me—I felt more forsaken than ever.

Chapter 6

(S)hattered

It was a fall evening—the kind where the air outside grows crisp and carries the faint, earthy scent of decaying leaves. Shadows stretched long, skeletal fingers across the lawn even before dinner was on the table. Inside, the familiar, comforting sounds of my parents getting ready filled the house—the soft thud of footsteps on the green-and-yellow linoleum of the kitchen floor, the low murmur of their voices discussing logistics, the clink of dishes as Mom hurriedly put dinner away and I cleared the table. They were planning to attend an evening session at the LDS temple, a regular commitment that usually meant one of the familiar teenage babysitters from the neighborhood would arrive soon, smelling faintly of bubble gum or cheap perfume, ready to oversee our bedtime routine.

But tonight, the usual well-oiled plan unraveled. Our regular sitter canceled at the last minute. I lingered near the kitchen doorway, pretending to be occupied with a small plastic doll, but really half-listening, my own small anxieties beginning to stir as Mom worked the phone. Her voice, usually soft, grew tighter, laced with an audible frustration with each unsuccessful call.

"Sorry, busy tonight."
"Oh, I wish I could, but..."
"Can't make it."

The list of available girls in the neighborhood seemed to shrink with each resigned sigh and the decisive click of the receiver being placed back in its cradle. My younger sisters were nearby, perhaps in the living room playing with blocks, their laughter a stark contrast to the mounting tension I felt radiating from the kitchen—blissfully unaware of the looming babysitter crisis that was causing Mom's shoulders to slump.

Then, drifting from the other room where Dad was, I heard one of them mention his name—my grandfather.

My sisters, hearing it too, might have perked up; they genuinely loved Grandpa, looked forward to his visits filled with silly jokes and maybe a piece of hard candy snuck from his pocket. They were completely innocent of the dark, suffocating reality I lived with whenever he was around. He wasn't abusing them. And certainly, no one else in our orbit knew he was abusing me. My secret was heavy and poisonous—a burden he forced me to carry with the chilling threat:

"If you tell anyone, YOU will be in big trouble".

But for me, just the sound of his name being spoken aloud as a possibility hit like a physical blow. A cold dread, sharp and sickeningly familiar, washed over me, instantly rooting me to the spot in the narrow kitchen hallway. The patterned linoleum and the slightly peeling paint on the walls suddenly felt like they were closing in, the space constricting around my chest. My breath hitched in my throat—a silent gasp—and my small hands began to tremble, a tremor that quickly radiated through my entire body. I froze, trapped between the wall and the doorframe, utterly alone in my secret terror.

No. Please no. Not him. Anyone but him.

The thought of it made my stomach churn.

The abuse—his secret touches that felt like spiders crawling on my skin, his whispered threats that echoed in my nightmares—had already cast a long, dark cloud over my young life for what felt like an eternity, though it had probably been months, maybe a year or more. It was escalating, growing bolder, more invasive, more terrifying with each forced encounter, each "special time" he engineered. The thought of him being here, in the perceived safety of our own house, alone with us—but really, alone with me, in my nighttime vulnerability, in my own bed—for hours while my parents were gone... it conjured suffocating images of his face, his hands, his scent, and raw fears I couldn't bear to fully form in my mind.

A desperate, primal certainty surged within me—a chilling knowledge no eight-year-old should possess: If he came over tonight, it would be worse than ever before. He would take advantage of the opportunity, the lack of supervision, the darkness.

And alongside the familiar terror, a new feeling flickered—faint but insistent: exhaustion.

A bone-deep weariness that settled in my small limbs. I couldn't take it anymore. I couldn't keep pretending, couldn't keep carrying this alone, couldn't keep the secret that felt like it was eating me from the inside out. I couldn't survive another night like the ones I feared were coming—especially not while trying to act normal, to protect my sisters from a danger they didn't even know existed.

It felt like hours standing there in the hallway, paralyzed by a fear so profound it seemed to steal the very air from my lungs, leaving me dizzy and nauseous. My heart hammered against my ribs—a frantic drumbeat against the sudden, ringing silence in my ears.

Don't let them call him. Please, Heavenly Father, don't let them call him.

But even as I prayed, a part of me knew it was likely too late, that the decision was being made.

Then, somehow, from a place deep inside I didn't know existed, a fragile, desperate tendril of courage emerged. It wasn't bravery—not the kind you read about in stories with heroes. It was the sheer, visceral inability to endure one more second of this torment, this crushing weight of dread. It was self-preservation kicking in when compliance felt like certain death to my spirit. My small body felt heavy with the secret, yet light with a strange, new resolve.

Summoning every ounce of that desperate, shaky strength, I forced my trembling legs to move. Each step down the familiar linoleum hallway toward my parents' bedroom felt heavy, deliberate—like wading through thick, invisible mud. The doorknob of their closed door felt cold and enormous under my small, clammy hand. I pushed it open.

They looked up from where they were getting dressed, their expressions a mixture of surprise and perhaps slight annoyance at the interruption. Mom was buttoning her dress; Dad was tying his tie.

The dam broke. My secret poured out in halting whispers. What my grandpa—my dad's dad—had been doing to me.

The moments immediately after my confession are a confusing blur in my memory, like looking through a rain-streaked window. I don't recall their exact expressions—was it shock? Disbelief? Anger? Or a confusing mix of all three? Perhaps they hugged me. Perhaps they asked questions, their voices hushed and strange.

What remains etched in my memory, with a chilling, baffling clarity that haunts me to this day, is the ultimate outcome: they still left.

After hearing the horrific secret their daughter had finally summoned the courage to reveal—after the tears and the whispered horrors—they still went to the temple. They somehow managed to find a younger girl from the neighborhood, someone barely older than me, perhaps ten or eleven, to come over and watch us while they were gone. They called my grandpa and told him not to come, that plans had changed.

But then they walked out the door.

As a child, all I could register was the hollow ache of their absence. I had finally spoken the truth, and still, they walked out the door. That night branded me with a deep unease around waiting—especially waiting after sharing something vulnerable. Even now, decades later, the anticipation that follows disclosure can make my skin buzz and my chest tighten, as though I'm bracing for abandonment all over again.

As an adult, I've learned the rest of the story. My mom told me she needed to be in a place of peace to process what I had said. I can understand that now, and I don't hold bitterness toward her for it. But understanding does not erase the impact. Trauma can live on in the body long after forgiveness takes root. You can let go of anger and still honor the fact that a moment wounded you.

The house felt vast and terrifyingly empty after they closed the front door behind them—the click of the lock echoing like a gunshot. I was alone with my sisters, the young, unprepared babysitter, and the crushing weight of what I'd just revealed hanging in the air like toxic dust.

Did they not believe me?
Was the temple more important than what I just said?
Was I truly alone in this?

The questions began their relentless assault—questions that would echo for decades.

The next day dawned heavy and uncertain, the air in the house thick with unspoken tension. Breakfast was quiet, strained. My parents went to confront my grandfather. I waited at home, suspended in a state of anxious limbo, unable to eat, unable to play, my stomach twisting into painful knots. Time stretched and warped.

What would he say? Would they believe him over me?

The fear of that was almost as bad as the abuse itself.

They returned later, their faces carefully neutral, unreadable.

He had denied it, they told me, their voices calm, conveying the information almost clinically. He'd tried to dismiss my account entirely, painting himself as innocent—claiming he was only "rubbing my belly" in a playful, grandfatherly gesture. Then came the question that made my stomach clench—the words that felt like a betrayal, even if unintended:

"Are you sure, Amber? Could you have been mistaken?"

Mistaken?

How could I mistake that feeling? That violation? That fear? The scent of his musk cologne when he held me too close?

But the raw certainty from the night before—the desperate courage born of exhaustion—hadn't faded. It was lodged deep within me, an undeniable, visceral truth.

"No," I insisted, my voice small but suddenly firm, cutting through my fear, my gaze steady on theirs. "I'm not mistaken."

I held onto the story I had finally dared to speak aloud, refusing to let it be erased, explained away, or minimized.

Armed with my unwavering account, my parents returned to confront my grandfather again. This time, faced with the unshakeable conviction of a child who would not back down—whose story held the ring of terrible truth—he confessed.

He admitted it.

And just like that, with his admission, the very foundations of my world didn't just crumble—they exploded.

The ground shifted beneath my feet, becoming unstable and treacherous. Everything I thought I knew about safety, family, trust, and love—everything that had once felt solid and predictable—was suddenly unrecognizable.

The confession didn't bring relief; it brought chaos.

It forced me to face a terrifying, fractured reality: the monsters weren't just under my bed—they were in my home, around my dinner table, wearing familiar faces and names I was taught to trust.

It wasn't only my grandfather's betrayal that shattered me—it was the way others left me unprotected, the way silence wrapped itself around the truth, the way love became conditional on my compliance.

This moment cracked open a truth I would spend years unraveling:

That the trauma didn't end with him.

It multiplied.

It morphed.

And it followed me.

CHAPTER 7

(E)mpty

In the days after my disclosure, life didn't suddenly shift the way I thought it might. My parents still went to the temple, still carried on with the rhythms of our faith, as if keeping those commitments could somehow steady the ground beneath us.

When my confirmation came, I wanted to believe it would mark a change—a moment where the Holy Ghost might actually wrap me in the comfort I'd been promised. Instead, I sat under the weight of a dozen hands, listening to the words spoken over me, and felt... nothing.

That emptiness lingered. In the months—perhaps even years— that followed, life outside of my internal turmoil felt like a confusing, disjointed blur. The foundation of our extended family, which had once seemed so solid, cracked and splintered. My grandparents divorced—an unthinkable event that shattered the hub of our family life. The brown brick house was no longer a place of automatic gathering. My grandfather moved in with his parents—my great-grandparents—just one house separating him from Grandma, his proximity a constant, painful, and unavoidable reminder of the brokenness of the secret I had carried.

The only aunt I had felt particularly close to got married and moved far away, extinguishing another source of potential comfort and understanding. The big, boisterous family get-togethers—the holiday traditions that had defined my childhood—ceased to exist as I had known them. The life I thought was immutable was gone, replaced by awkward silences, fractured relationships, and an unspoken tension that hung in the air whenever certain family members were present.

And through it all, the silent yet resounding message from many of those around me—conveyed through averted gazes at family dinners, quick changes of subject if anything uncomfortable arose, and a general atmosphere of forced cheerfulness—was clear:
Get over it. Move on. Don't talk about it. Sweep this so far under the rug that it can never, ever resurface.

But how could I?

The conflict raged inside me, especially within the walls of the church building each Sunday. The lessons on forgiveness felt like personal attacks, each word a fresh stab of guilt.
If you don't forgive, you will go to hell.

Those weren't the exact words spoken from the pulpit or by my Sunday School teacher—whether it was Brother Smith or any of the other adults who rotated through teaching us. Before I disclosed, these were people I respected, parents of my friends, adults whose approval I valued. But after I told the secret—whether they actually knew or not—their eyes felt different to me. It was as if they could see the stain I carried, as if they were silently judging me for not forgiving, for being "dirty," and worst of all, for speaking a secret I wasn't supposed to tell.

That's how their words translated in my young, preteen-into-teen mind—already heavy with guilt that was never mine to carry.

How? The question screamed inside me during one particular lesson, the image of my grandfather's face flashing in my mind. *How am I supposed to forgive him if he has never apologized?*

My hand shot up, trembling slightly, my palm sweaty. "Brother Smith?" My voice sounded small, reedy, in the quiet classroom filled with other children who seemed so untroubled. "How am I supposed to forgive someone who hasn't apologized?"

His response was frustratingly generic—a well-rehearsed platitude I felt I'd heard countless times before. His smile didn't quite reach his eyes as he referenced a scripture, something about how the Lord will forgive whom He chooses, but that it is commanded of us—the victims, the hurt ones—to forgive all.

No nuance.

No acknowledgment of the complexities of trauma or the need for accountability from the one who caused the harm.

Just a divine commandment I felt utterly incapable of fulfilling—a spiritual burden too heavy for my small shoulders.

So I'm going to hell? The thought was terrifying—a cold dread spreading through me. *Me? I didn't hurt him. He hurt me. He isn't even sorry! But I'm the one going to hell?!*

It felt profoundly unjust, another layer of blame heaped upon my already overburdened conscience. Tears started to well, hot and stinging, blurring the image of the flannel-graph Jesus on the board. I couldn't sit there a moment longer—couldn't bear the weight of the judgment, both divine and perceived from the adults around me.

I mumbled a request to be excused from class, my voice choked. Rushing out of the classroom—past the sympathetic but uncomprehending gaze of Brother Smith and toward the heavy front doors of the church—my only hope was that one of my parents or another watchful adult from the ward wouldn't try to stop me, wouldn't drag me back into that suffocating atmosphere.

I just couldn't be there.

Once my parents found out I'd left church early, I knew I was going to be grounded—probably for a week or more—but even that punishment felt preferable to sitting in that classroom, drowning in guilt and injustice.

Later that day, the inevitable confrontation arrived.
"Amber, you know the rules in this house..." my dad began, his voice stern, his disappointment a palpable weight in the room.

I know, I know, I thought miserably, staring at my shoes. *I don't get a say in this. It's so stupid!* My feelings, my pain, didn't seem to matter; church attendance was mandatory.

"I don't want to be there!" I finally yelled, the frustration and despair boiling over. I turned and slammed my bedroom door shut, the sound echoing my internal explosion. I jumped onto my bed, burying my face in my pillow, bracing myself for the footsteps I knew were coming down the hall.

"Don't you slam this door!" he yelled, bursting into my room just as I'd expected.

A quick, hard smack landed on my butt, stinging through my clothes—a punctuation mark to my misery.

"It's not fair," I sobbed into the bedding, the words muffled. "I hate it there. Everyone hates me!"

"No one hates you," he said, his voice perhaps softening slightly, but still firm—unable to bridge the chasm of my despair.
"Don't come out of this room until dinner time."

The door clicked shut, leaving me alone with my overwhelming, suffocating thoughts.
They all hate me. The thought circled relentlessly. *Everything is my fault. I ruined our family. They blame me for everything!*

The weight of it all felt crushing. Unbearable.

Defeated and overwhelmed, my small body shaking with sobs, I dragged myself to my little desk. I grabbed a pencil and tore a sheet of paper from my unicorn-themed notebook. In shaky, childish handwriting—the pencil lead sometimes tearing the thin paper—I poured out my anguish:

I want to die. Please, I want to. I love you but it seems like everybody is against me. I hate it. I want to die.

My hand trembling, I slid the note under my closed bedroom door—a desperate, silent plea into the empty hallway.
A cry for help I didn't know how else to make.

CHAPTER 8

(I)njustice

While I was drowning in questions about forgiveness, worthiness, and whether anyone truly saw me beyond my secret, the adults around me were moving into another arena entirely—one I couldn't enter, much less understand. The conversations at home grew quieter, the glances more guarded. Words like charges and court began floating through the air, foreign and heavy.

Following my grandfather's confession, grown-ups spoke in hushed, serious tones, their voices low as if the very words might burn if spoken too loudly. It felt like something big and ominous was happening—something centered on what my grandfather had done—yet it was all happening without me. I was far too young to grasp the gravity of the situation, let alone the intricate dance of law and consequence. The weight of it all—the raw betrayal, the broken trust, the swirling, complex adult emotions that filled our house like a thick fog—was simply incomprehensible to my nine-year-old mind.

Despite his admission of what he'd done, my grandfather was never arrested, never taken away in a police car like I'd seen on television. Instead, formal charges were filed—I believe they may have initially been serious felony charges, though the specifics were a blur of adult jargon to me then—and he was given a court date. The whole process felt abstract, something happening to him, a consequence he had to face. But it didn't feel like it was happening *for me*—the little girl whose world he had violated.

Then, my parents informed me that I would need to attend his hearing.

"Just in case the judge wishes to speak with you", they said, their tone attempting reassurance.

The prospect filled me with a cold, churning dread.
What would I say?
Would I have to see him?
Would they make me tell the story again in front of strangers?

The unknown loomed, heavy and terrifying.

I remember accompanying my dad to the local City Courthouse. It was a building I had only ever known as the one next door to the public library—a place of colorful picture books, puppet shows, and the gentle rustle of turning pages. But now, it felt imposing, official, and cold.

The hallway leading toward the courtroom seemed to stretch for miles. The dark brown brick walls weren't just dark—they were shiny, almost wet-looking, like they'd been coated in epoxy. They caught and reflected the overhead lights in strange, warped glimmers, as if the building itself were trying to stay polished while holding so much heaviness inside. The air felt too still, sterile. The floor gleamed beneath our feet, so highly polished I could almost see my reflection, distorted and ghostlike.

Every sound was amplified.
The sharp click of my dad's dress shoes.
The anxious shuffle of my small feet.
The echo of a door closing somewhere down the corridor.
The distant, unintelligible murmur of adult voices.

Each footstep felt like a drumbeat, marching me toward something I desperately wanted to avoid.

We didn't go inside the courtroom immediately. We sat on a hard, wooden bench in the hallway—the kind that felt too big for me, my feet dangling far above the floor. The air smelled faintly of floor wax and old paper. I watched other people walk past—men in suits carrying briefcases, women with worried expressions—all moving with a purpose I didn't understand. I felt small, out of place—a child in a world of serious adult business. The anticipation and my unnamed fear gnawed at me, making my stomach feel tight and queasy.

I was never called in to speak.

My dad, however, was eventually summoned. I remember him standing up, straightening his tie, his face unreadable, and walking through the heavy courtroom doors, leaving me alone on that hard bench. The sense of isolation was profound.

What were they saying in there?
Why wasn't I needed?
Did they believe me?
Was he going to get in big trouble like he deserved?

The questions swirled, unanswered, in my young, confused mind.

Years later, long after the event itself had faded into the confusing tapestry of childhood memory, I would discover the devastating truth about what transpired during that hearing—while I waited alone in the hall, tracing patterns in the linoleum with the toe of my shoe.

My dad had *not* gone into that courtroom to demand justice for his daughter—the child whose trust had been so horrifically violated by his own father. Instead, he had gone in to plead for mercy for his father. My abuser. He had asked the judge for leniency.

His plea was granted.

As part of a deal, the charges my grandfather ultimately faced were reduced to two counts of misdemeanor lewdness in the presence of a child. And even then, he was offered—and accepted—a plea in abeyance. This meant that upon his completion of a year of therapy and probation, the legal slate would be wiped clean. The charges would be dismissed.

As if the abuse had never occurred.
As if my pain, my stolen innocence, didn't warrant a lasting record of his crime.

This injustice became the faulty foundation upon which my sense of self, my understanding of the world, and my place within my family was built. And it would not be the last time I'd watch those around me—family and community—choose the comfort of denial over the truth. The next chapter of my life would prove that even the ending of a court case doesn't end the story.

CHAPTER 9

(F)ractured

The court hearing was over, but nothing felt resolved. Instead of closure, I was left with a jagged landscape of altered relationships and quiet betrayals. The ground beneath my feet—once steady in the rhythm of extended family life—was permanently unstable. And then, less than two years later, he got engaged. The very day his probation ended.

The casualness of it—how seamlessly he transitioned into a new chapter—was jarring. And gutting. It was as if none of it had happened. His ability to move forward only amplified the message I was already internalizing: *He gets a clean slate. You get to carry the wreckage.*

He and his new wife bought a house less than a mile away from our home. It had a pool in the backyard and became a popular neighborhood gathering spot. Their blended family appeared whole, untouched by the trauma he left behind. Most people didn't know.

The children certainly didn't. And I would see them—splashing, laughing, running in swimsuits under his supervision—while I sat with the memory of what he had done. It felt surreal. While I carried the weight of his abuse every day, he floated above consequence.

Therapists—most of whom I never chose—and church leaders echoed the same sentiment: "Keep the family together." That was the priority. And while no one explicitly said I should be the only one in therapy, that's how it played out. Session after session, it was just me sitting in the chair, week after week, learning early on to see myself as the problem that needed fixing.

We continued to see my grandfather regularly. Family events, holidays, birthday parties. I was expected to show up, to be polite, to act normal. My trauma became something I had to manage quietly so that others could remain comfortable. My younger siblings still loved him, unaware or unwilling to accept the truth of what he'd done. And while I was navigating trauma responses and internal chaos, they laughed at his jokes and sat on his lap. Their innocence, their continued bond with him, was painful to watch. It isolated me further.

My mother, to her credit, refused to attend his second wedding. It was the firmest boundary she'd drawn. But my father went. Maybe he felt obligated. Maybe he couldn't stomach the discomfort of fully cutting ties. Maybe it was about image. I don't know. But his decision to attend felt like a betrayal—a continuation of the same pattern: loyalty to the abuser, not the abused.

This split in my immediate family mirrored the fractures throughout the rest of our extended family. I didn't know how to trust anyone anymore. And I didn't know what healing was supposed to look like when the world around me kept insisting that nothing had really happened.

Being around my grandfather and his new wife was a bewildering experience of contradictions. Her constant comments about my weight, always framed as concern or compliments—"Have you lost weight?" —cut like paper. At the time, I didn't see it for what it was: control. Undermining. A way to keep me small. A way to compete for his attention, which she viewed as a prize.

Later, she admitted she'd known "something." But she "didn't want to delve." That refusal, that willful ignorance, was its own form of violence. Her loyalty was to the version of him she wanted to believe in—not the truth that would have required her to confront the monster in her home. I wasn't a person to her. I was a threat to her illusion.

I remember a family BBQ when I was around fourteen or fifteen. I was jumping on the trampoline, trying to feel normal, trying to forget. My shorts snagged on a spring and tore, exposing more of me than I intended. I cried—not just from embarrassment, but from a much deeper humiliation. My abuser saw me. His wife saw me. And I saw her watching me with an expression I would later understand: not concern. Not compassion. Something colder.

Back then, I still craved his approval. I still believed, on some level, that if I was good enough, quiet enough, small enough, maybe I'd be accepted. Maybe they'd love me. That desperation made me easy to manipulate. My compliance—my silence—was mistaken for forgiveness. Adults around us interpreted it as proof that we were moving on. That things were "better."

They weren't better. They were repressed. They were buried. And I was slowly disappearing underneath them.

In time, more pieces of his character came into focus. He had been a businessman—respected, maybe even admired by some—but his ventures were riddled with dishonesty. Broken promises. Shady dealings. People were left in financial ruin. My grandmother, his ex-wife, got virtually nothing in the divorce.

When he eventually died, there was no inheritance. No gesture of acknowledgment. No attempt to make anything right.

His legacy, for me, wasn't business savvy or patriarchal strength. It was destruction.
It was betrayal.
It was me, clawing my way through the wreckage he left behind, trying to figure out how to build something true out of everything he broke.

This period, from the court hearing until my late teens, was a confusing landscape of conflicting advice, fractured family loyalty, forced interactions, and the constant, gnawing awareness of the injustice that allowed my abuser to maintain a facade of normalcy while I struggled with the invisible wounds. The trauma lingered, a persistent ache, resurfacing in unexpected ways, shaping my interactions, my view of myself, and my understanding of the world as I navigated the difficult terrain of adolescence under the heavy shadow of unresolved abuse. It wouldn't be until my grandfather's health began to seriously fail, as I stood on the cusp of adulthood myself, that this particular chapter of interacting with him, and the specific pain it entailed, would draw to its inevitable close.

CHAPTER 10

(C)oward

The memory of the day my grandfather passed away is etched in my mind, starting with the moment I stepped into the hospital elevator. The air inside the small car was stale, thick with the institutional smell of disinfectant and unspoken anxieties. A wave of dread washed over me—a physical pressure, as if it were pushing me back against the elevator's upward pull.

As the doors slid open onto his floor with a soft ding, the hallway stretched before me, unnaturally quiet except for the distant beep of machinery and the hushed voices of nurses. Time seemed to slow to an agonizing crawl. Each step on the polished linoleum felt heavy, as if my feet were encased in cement, the squeak of my shoes echoing too loudly in the stillness. A strong, visceral urge to turn and run—to flee back to the noise and normalcy of the outside world—consumed me.

He doesn't deserve this, I thought, the words a bitter refrain in my mind. *He doesn't deserve to be surrounded by loved ones in his final moments after what he did.* The tears welling in my eyes weren't for him—not for the man lying frail in a hospital bed—they were for me. For the years of unresolved anger. For the deep well of despair that churned within me.

All I had ever truly needed from him was a genuine acknowledgment, a simple expression of remorse for the pain he had caused. But that couldn't happen if I wasn't even willing to be in the room—to face him one last time.

I forced myself to walk toward his room, my heart pounding a frantic rhythm against my ribs, yet I couldn't bring myself to cross the threshold. I remained just outside the doorway, a silent, conflicted sentinel—close enough for my parents to find me if he somehow asked for me, but far enough away to avoid seeing him, to avoid confronting the complex storm of emotions his presence, even in weakness, evoked. The turmoil within me raged on, a constant battle between the lingering, childish desire for some impossible closure and the overwhelming weight of righteous resentment.

What happened next is blurred in my memory. I don't remember being called in. I don't remember leaving the hospital. I don't even remember hearing the words that he had died. My body tells me it may have been that day, but my mind only offers fragments. The next clear image is of myself sitting alone in my bedroom in the days before his funeral, telling myself I could forgive him.

It wasn't for him. It was for me. I convinced myself I could let go, that I didn't need an apology to move forward. In that moment, I felt a weight lift off my shoulders, a strange lightness filling the space where rage had been. I told myself I was healed. I even believed it—

until his funeral just days later, and the events that followed, proved otherwise.

His death was not sudden; it was a drawn-out process marked by his deteriorating health, offering no solace or sense of justice to me. While some might find a grim comfort in the belief that he experienced physical suffering, it did nothing to ease my own internal pain. His physical decline didn't equate to atonement in my eyes. And while others in the periphery of our fractured family might perhaps revel in the thought of him facing eternal damnation, it brought me no satisfaction. I felt I had already endured a lifetime of undeserved torment—a personal hell forged by his actions and the subsequent fallout, which had left its indelible mark on my soul.

He was a coward, and he died a coward's death. He never sought my forgiveness, never uttered a single word of apology for the devastation he had wrought upon my childhood, upon my family. He left this world long before I found the strength within myself to truly confront him as an adult—to articulate the depths of the pain, the anger, the confusion he had inflicted upon my soul. His passing extinguished any lingering hope I held onto for healing to come through him—for some grand gesture or heartfelt confession that would magically make things right.

That's what I believed, at least, for a long, long time—that his lack of remorse, his silence even unto death, sealed my fate, leaving me permanently damaged and forever denied the acknowledgement I craved.

The experience of his funeral a few days later was surreal, like walking through a dream I couldn't wake from. The church was filled with familiar faces—many of whom knew parts of the story, or at least sensed that something was deeply wrong. As I sat numbly in the hard wooden pew, the air thick with the scent of lilies and old hymn books, listening to members of his new family extol his virtues—his kindness, his generosity, his quiet strength—a wave of disbelief and quiet rage washed over me.

Their words felt like a profound betrayal, a willful distortion of the man I knew, the man whose actions had caused such irreparable harm. It was like attending the funeral of a stranger—a carefully constructed character who happened to wear my grandfather's face. Each glowing tribute felt like a fresh invalidation of my experience, a collective agreement to remember only the good, to erase the monstrous.

Despite my inner turmoil, the suffocating feeling of unreality, I couldn't stay away entirely. The funeral was a gathering of almost everyone I held dear—my entire fractured family assembled in one place. A part of me, perhaps the wounded child still within, yearned for solace—for someone, anyone, to acknowledge the depth of my pain and confusion. To see the dissonance between the man being eulogized and the reality I carried in my bones.

Instead, I felt utterly isolated and profoundly misunderstood—adrift in a sea of performative grief that didn't match my own complex sorrow, which was more a grief for my lost childhood and the family that could have been than for the man himself.

Overwhelmed by emotion—anger at the sanitized narrative, sadness for the little girl who was never protected, confusion at the polite smiles and hushed condolences—I left the service halfway through. I couldn't bear to hear another word. I sought refuge in the quiet, empty foyer, the sounds of the organ and the eulogy muffled by the closed doors.

As I sat there alone on a plush chair, trying to compose myself, trying to breathe through the tightness in my chest, I couldn't shake the feeling that I was being judged. The whispers I imagined, the sideways glances I felt from those who noticed my departure, seemed to confirm my worst fears: that I was being perceived as dramatic, attention-seeking, selfish for not being able to sit quietly and mourn the sanitized version of the man they chose to remember.

This perception—whether real or imagined—haunted me for years, casting a long shadow over my grief. It reinforced the insidious message that my pain was an inconvenience, an unwelcome disruption to the family narrative—something best kept hidden.

CHAPTER 11

(R)ebellion

What came next wasn't healing. It was a slow slide into chaos—messy, defiant, and disguised as freedom. I had convinced myself that forgiving my grandfather meant I was "over it," but in reality, I was just skilled at hiding the parts of me that weren't.

The foundation laid by the abuse, the silence afterward, and my father's firm command that it never be spoken of again created an internal pressure cooker. There was no safe outlet for the pain or the anger. Every attempt to speak up—whether about what had happened or how I was feeling—was met with conflict, punishment, or cold dismissal. Silence became my survival tactic.

Layered on top of that was the weight of religious expectation. Inside the church, I was taught about purity, forgiveness, and worthiness, yet I carried the sting of feeling unseen by God, and the resentment of a system that asked more of the victim than the perpetrator. It was a double standard I couldn't untangle.

Unable to reconcile those contradictions, I started telling myself a story that I thought might save me: maybe the abuse hadn't hurt me as badly as I thought. Maybe I could rise above it, prove I wasn't a victim at all. If that was true, then my rebellion wasn't a cry for help— it was just who I was. A "bad kid." In some warped way, taking all the blame felt like control.

That belief pushed me toward a frantic search for validation, most often through relationships. I wanted to be wanted. I wanted to feel chosen. And when the attention I craved didn't come from the people I hoped it would, I took whatever scraps were offered and tried to make them feel like enough.

Growing up, I was never the prettiest or the skinniest in my friend group. The boys I liked rarely liked me back. The ones who did notice me were usually hoping to get closer to one of my friends. Even as far back as fourth grade, my attempts at "relationships" had ended in embarrassment and rejection, each one quietly adding to the belief that I wasn't worth wanting.

That year I met Marie. She understood me in ways no one else did—because she had also been sexually abused. Her house, often empty of adults, became our hideout. We'd talk in hushed tones about things we couldn't say anywhere else, our secrets wrapped in the smell of her mom's perfume and laundry that never seemed quite clean. It was the first time I could say the truth out loud without fear.

Our circle of friends gathered there often, the most popular boys and girls in school, the air buzzing with adolescent energy. We played truth or dare and other games that gave the illusion of romance, but they mostly left me feeling like an outsider to the real thing. While my friends had stolen kisses and private moments with the boys they liked, I was often paired with whoever was "left," my heart sinking as I smiled and played along.

By junior high, I wanted so badly to feel chosen that I ignored the small voice inside me that whispered when something didn't feel right. Sometimes I froze. Sometimes I went along to avoid conflict. The lines between choice and pressure blurred until I could barely tell them apart.

Each time a rumor spread, my reputation shifted a little more. Boys who hadn't noticed me before suddenly did, but not for the reasons I wanted. I began saying yes when I wanted to say no, convincing myself it was easier. I didn't have the skills—or the belief in my own worth—to set and hold boundaries.

By senior year, I'd tangled myself in situations I didn't know how to get out of. I confused attention with love, pressure with passion. In my mind, intimacy was the currency of affection, and I was constantly overpaying.

Then I met Peter. He was older, kind, and treated me with a gentleness I hadn't experienced before. Our first date felt like something out of a movie—he opened doors, paid for dinner, and made me laugh. At homecoming, I felt genuinely wanted, maybe for the first time.

But when he didn't push for physical intimacy right away, I couldn't make sense of it. My mind told me his patience meant disinterest. I tried to prove my worth the only way I knew how, and the harder I pushed, the further away he pulled.

That pattern—pushing away what I most wanted, clinging to what would hurt me—followed me into my next chapter. It didn't end with Peter. It became a blueprint for years of my life, bleeding into relationship after relationship, shaping the way I measured my worth and how I defined love.

The names and faces changed, but the rhythm stayed the same— urgency over steadiness, intensity over safety, and a constant chasing of the very people who would never truly choose me. The cycle became so familiar, I mistook it for connection.

It would take decades—and many chapters—to even recognize that pattern for what it was. And it would take one man, much later, to finally show me that love didn't have to be earned through suffering.

But that revelation was still years away.

CHAPTER 12

(C)haos

The grief following my grandfather's death was complicated—tangled with anger, unfinished business, and a void where an apology should have been. Life, especially teenage life with its relentless forward momentum, marched on. December came just two months after his passing, and although the holidays came and went, nothing about them felt whole. I was technically an adult now, still in high school but with that new legal status, and the combination made me both restless and reckless.

I was still carrying the "bad kid" identity I'd adopted years before, still aching for validation, still desperate to feel seen. That combination made me an easy candidate for impulsive, destructive decisions. And one night, in a sticky vinyl booth at the fast-food restaurant where I worked, that volatility found its outlet.

The conversation started as a joke—how easy it would be to rob the place. There were no security cameras, the back door was often propped open, and as night-shift supervisor, I had access to the cash. But somewhere between laughter and boredom, the idea started to feel less like a joke and more like a plan.

A few nights later, it happened. I sent the other employees home early, stayed behind, and waited for my friend Chad to show up in black clothes and a ski mask. He took the cash from the till, grabbed a customer's camera from the office, then tied my wrists loosely with a rope and locked me in the walk-in fridge. I rubbed my wrists against the rope, making sure there'd be marks, then "escaped" and called 911, my voice shaking with rehearsed fear.

The police response was overwhelming—cars filling the parking lot, radios crackling, lights flashing against the windows. They photographed my wrists, took my statement, and asked for details I made up on the spot. My dad came to take me home, unaware that the "victim" story was a complete fabrication.

The local paper called me a hero the next day. People I barely knew told me how brave I was. For a moment, I had what I'd been chasing for years: attention, admiration, proof that I mattered. But beneath the surface, the guilt was immediate, heavy, and growing.

When Chad went on to rob two more places—one of them the same restaurant in broad daylight, with a gun pointed at someone I knew—the weight became unbearable. I went to my dad, told him about Chad and the later robberies, but left out my part in the first one. My dad took the information to the police. It turned out they already suspected us, and soon I was sitting in an interrogation room, telling the truth about my role.

The detectives promised I'd avoid jail if I cooperated, so I pleaded guilty to two misdemeanors: falsifying information and employee theft. What I didn't know—what no one explained—was that I should have had a lawyer. Once again, I was left to navigate something huge and terrifying on my own. The only guidance I was given was to "just tell the truth."

When I stood before the judge, I expected the deal I'd been promised. Instead, he sentenced me to twenty-one days in jail, a $1,200 fine, and full restitution. I was stunned. My dad sat in the courtroom, silent. Maybe because I was old enough now, and because this was something I had done, he thought it was best I face the full weight of the consequences.

By the time I served my sentence, it was eight months later—after my high school graduation and my senior trip. It was work release, but my job hours were cut, so I spent most of my time behind bars anyway. Eighteen days in jail feels like forever when you've never been there before. The boredom, the humiliation, the way it stripped away even the smallest illusions of control—it all left a mark.

Not long after, my car was set on fire outside the sandwich shop where I worked. A group of old classmates pulled into the drive-thru to tell me, and I ran outside to see the flames already consuming it. I called 911, but by the time the fire was out, it was totaled. The police claimed it was probably kids tossing a sparkler, but I couldn't shake the feeling it was connected to Chad's arrest.

I had no insurance that would cover the damage, no money for a tow, and no help from my employer. It was one more thing lost in a year already full of loss.

I stood in the parking lot that night, staring at the blackened shell, feeling the full weight of it—how quickly chaos could snowball, how far the ripples of one bad decision could reach.

And even then, I didn't see how these moments—the shame, the isolation, the quiet belief that I had to handle everything alone—would follow me for years. How they would shape the way I trusted, the way I connected. How they would push me into a pattern of extremes—keeping people at arm's length until I couldn't bear the distance, then clinging far too tightly once they got close.

CHAPTER 13

(E)scape

After serving eighteen days in jail, the immediate reality of post-high school life hit hard. My sister and I moved into an apartment together—a tentative step toward independence—but my job at the local sandwich shop wasn't going to cover my share of the expenses. The constant smell of baking bread and deli meats, once just part of the job, now felt like a reminder of my limited prospects.

I started looking for something, anything, that paid better and landed a position at a sprawling call center. The atmosphere there was a stark contrast—rows upon rows of cubicles under harsh fluorescent lights, the constant low hum of hundreds of voices on the phone, a feeling of anonymity that was both comforting and soul-crushing. This job turned out to be significant, not for the career path it offered, but because it's where I met Mitch.

He was older—mid-twenties—which I found attractive, projecting an air of maturity I lacked. When I realized he was flirting with me during breaks, I was overjoyed. After years of feeling inadequate and overlooked, the attention was flattering, intoxicating even, a balm to my bruised ego. I was excited, perhaps desperately so, to see where things might go.

Our relationship ignited quickly, marked by an intense and passionate connection that felt overwhelming and validating, filling the void I constantly felt. So when he revealed a few weeks into our relationship that he was married but claimed to be in the process of getting a divorce, I didn't think much of it. In my mind, skewed by a desperate need for affection and validation, the fact that he was choosing me, showering me with attention, seemed like all that mattered. The red flags were waving, but I was colorblind to them, blinded by the temporary high of feeling wanted.

However, the reality was far harsher, and the crash was inevitable. He wasn't truly choosing me, and there was no divorce on the horizon. The relationship ended as abruptly and intensely as it had begun, leaving a trail of destruction, shame, and self-loathing in its wake.

During this tumultuous period, the consequences rippled outward, pulling my family back into my chaos. My father, perhaps overwhelmed with concern, perhaps motivated by disappointment or even shame after my recent legal troubles—or perhaps driven by his pattern of wanting to see me face consequences while often overlooking the accountability of others—went to our bishop and disclosed my relationship with Mitch. Whatever his complex motivations, this act led directly to my being summoned for a bishop's council.

Sitting in that small, sterile office, facing five men from the ward leadership, their faces a mixture of pity and judgment, felt intensely intimidating. I recounted my recent transgressions, feeling exposed and ashamed under their gaze. The decision came swiftly: I was officially disfellowshipped from the church.

The public marking of my sin, the formal exclusion from the community (by way of not being able to offer up a public prayer or hold a church calling, amongst other restrictions) I had known my whole life, compounded the shame and isolation I felt. Adrift in a sea of despair, overwhelmed by the judgment, the wreckage of the relationship, and now the condemnation of my church, I felt an urgent, suffocating need to escape. I made the difficult decision to leave Utah, needing physical distance from the pain, the judgment, and the constant reminders of my mistakes.

The search for an escape route led me to online listings for nanny positions outside of Utah. A family in Philadelphia with energetic eighteen-month-old triplets expressed interest. The prospect felt daunting but also like a clean slate. I accepted the position and began making preparations, packing the few belongings I had. Just as things were solidifying, another offer came through—a family in Florida with older children, offering the chance to travel the world and earn a higher salary. The allure of travel and better pay was tempting, a glimpse of a different kind of life. Despite this, I felt bound by my commitment to the Philadelphia family. Honoring my word felt important—perhaps one small way to counteract the recent chaos and instability. I decided to stick with the original plan.

So, in 2001, at the age of twenty, carrying a suitcase filled with clothes and a heart heavy with baggage, I embarked on a journey into the wider world, leaving the familiar mountains and valleys of Utah behind. I didn't consider myself overly sheltered or naive; I didn't anticipate being shocked by cultural differences. But boy, was I mistaken.

Arriving in Philadelphia felt like landing on a different planet. The pace was faster, the accents unfamiliar, the sheer diversity overwhelming. Even simple things—like watching people enjoy a glass of wine with dinner or seeing people casually smoking cigars—felt strange and foreign against the backdrop of my Mormon upbringing where such things were forbidden or frowned upon. I felt like an outsider observing a world that operated under different rules, acutely aware of my Utah roots, my differentness, in this new, unfamiliar place.

It wasn't long after moving to Philadelphia, while navigating the challenges of caring for three toddlers and adjusting to East Coast life, that I met Eric. We connected in an online chat room—a relatively new way to meet people back then. He seemed like a decent person from his messages—stable, kind, employed. Despite some disapproval from my parents and friends back home about the perceived dangers of meeting someone online, the loneliness of being in a new city was profound. I agreed to go out with him.

Our first date was a revelation in its normalcy and respectfulness. He picked me up at the family's house where I was living, arriving on time. He took me to Applebee's for dinner—nothing fancy, but comfortable. Afterwards, we went to a nearby park, the air cool and damp, and tossed a frisbee back and forth under the setting sun. The entire experience felt foreign in its simplicity and courtesy. Being formally asked out, picked up, having dinner paid for, having car doors opened—this wasn't the dynamic I was used to from my teenage relationships or the brief, intense encounters since. Eric was a gentleman, a rare find in my limited dating experience. It felt... nice. Safe, even.

I found him cute enough, with kind, deep-set eyes and a shy smile. More importantly, I genuinely appreciated his kindness, his respectfulness, his stable career, and the uncomplicated affection he showed me. In a new city where I knew virtually no one beyond the family I worked for, he quickly became my closest companion—a steady, reliable presence in my uncertain world.

Driven perhaps by my ingrained desire for commitment and security—the need to anchor myself after so much turmoil—it was me who first suggested we become a serious couple. Eric was initially hesitant, perhaps sensing my underlying neediness or simply wanting to take things slower. But I persuaded him, needing the label, the security of being someone's girlfriend. We made it official. Just a few months later, the trajectory of our relationship took a sharp, unexpected turn: I found out I was pregnant.

The first trimester was incredibly difficult. Constant, debilitating nausea and overwhelming fatigue made caring for the energetic triplets nearly impossible. The smell of formula, dirty diapers, even Eric's Curve cologne—a scent I had once liked—now made me sick. To this day, that smell makes me nauseous.

As the pregnancy progressed, the initial shock gave way to the daunting reality of impending motherhood. Eric wanted me to stay in Pennsylvania, envisioning us building a life there together, raising our child near his family and job. But the thought of facing childbirth, the pain and vulnerability of it, and the overwhelming responsibility of caring for a newborn so far from my family felt utterly impossible. I didn't have health insurance through the nanny job, and the financial burden of raising a baby largely on my own, even with Eric's support, terrified me. The combination of physical discomfort, emotional distress, profound homesickness, and gnawing financial worries solidified my decision: I needed to return home to Utah, to the safety net—however complicated—of my family.

Eric flew home with me to meet my family just before I officially moved back in. We booked separate flights, and he arrived earlier than I did. My dad, ever punctual, picked him up at the Salt Lake City airport. Later, Dad recounted their first meeting with a smirk. Eric, he said, was not what he'd expected—not necessarily in a bad way, just... different. With his small stature, slumped shoulders, and quiet demeanor, he didn't resemble the man my dad had envisioned his daughter ending up with. "Bit of a dork," Dad said, half-joking— though I knew he meant it.

During Eric's visit, we took a trip to the family cabin—a place that, for most of my family, was synonymous with sanctuary and tradition. And in many ways, it was for me too. I had plenty of fond memories: catching horned toads in dusty mason jars, building forts out of old refrigerator boxes, playing board games at the large kitchen table, watching movies under heavy quilts, swimming in the bracing cold of natural pools, and collapsing into laughter during makeshift leg wrestling matches. But despite all that joy, the cabin never felt entirely safe to me. Every time we turned off onto the long dirt road that led through the trees, a familiar tightness gripped my chest. Because no matter how fun a visit might have been, they were all forever overshadowed by the abuse that had taken place there.

One vivid memory—the only clear recollection I have of the abuse itself—happened at that cabin. My grandfather had convinced my parents to let me and my younger sister come with him. While she sat just a few feet in front of us, watching *Jaws* on the television, he pulled me onto his lap. The juxtaposition was haunting: the fictional terror of a great white shark on the screen, and the real, insidious danger happening behind it. To this day, *Jaws* holds a magnified terror for me. It's not just the suspense or the music—it's the memory of what was happening while it played, the feeling of being violated within reach of safety, the confusion of knowing something was deeply wrong but having no words or power to stop it.

The cabin, for me, became a symbol of that duality. The scent of pine needles and woodsmoke still carries both warmth and dread. It was a place where laughter echoed, but so did silence—the kind that hides secrets in the walls.

While at the cabin during Eric's visit, the mountain air crisp around us, he suggested we take a walk. Pregnant and easily exhausted, I initially declined, wanting only to rest. But he persisted gently, and my family, likely sensing his intentions, chimed in with encouragement—"Oh, go on, the fresh air will do you good!"—until I relented.

We strolled down the familiar dirt path toward the crick. When we reached it, he turned to me, took a deep breath, and knelt. His sunglasses reflected my own face back at me—rounder now from pregnancy, eyes shadowed by exhaustion. The world seemed to quiet around us, the water still, the breeze momentarily holding its breath.

In that pause, I felt it—an invisible weight pressing against my chest. This was supposed to be a moment of joy, but my body told a different story. My stomach tightened, not from the baby or the nausea, but from a truth I didn't want to name: I didn't love him, not in the way I felt I should. At the time, I couldn't understand why. Only much later, while doing the final read-through of this book, did I realize it was because he was safe—at least then. He wasn't the chaos or the chase I had grown so used to, the kind of volatility I confused for love. Back then, safety felt foreign—almost uncomfortable.

I wouldn't know until years later that the safety I felt in that moment would erode, replaced by something very different. But in that fall afternoon, standing in a place that held its own ghosts, I said yes. The word slipped out, soft and automatic. Part of me clung to the idea of stability—of not facing single motherhood alone. But beneath that yes was the quiet thrum of unease, a knowing that this wasn't the right choice.

Eric returned to Philadelphia after the visit. The plan was for me to give birth in Utah, and then we would get married and figure out our future. But the feeling that I had made the wrong choice didn't dissipate. It grew stronger, heavier, with each passing week of my pregnancy.

Ultimately, wrestling with my conflicting emotions—the desire for family support versus the commitment to a man I wasn't sure I truly loved—and the weight of the commitment I'd made under duress, I made the heart-wrenching decision to end our engagement before the wedding could even be planned. With a heavy heart, feeling both guilty and strangely liberated, I composed an email to Eric, typed the dreaded subject line *Dear John,* and, taking a deep breath, pressed send—severing the tie and plunging myself back into uncertainty, albeit an uncertainty that felt more honest than the path I had almost taken.

CHAPTER 14

(R)edemption

My first son, Scott, was born in 2002. The moment they placed his tiny, wrinkled body, warm and surprisingly heavy, into my arms, a wave of love unlike anything I had ever experienced washed over me—fierce, overwhelming, absolute. His small fingers curled around mine, and looking into his unfocused newborn eyes, the chaos and uncertainty of my own life seemed to momentarily recede. He had arrived when I felt utterly lost, uncertain about my identity, my desires, my future direction. Yet, in that instant, holding him close, smelling that unique newborn scent of milk and powder, I felt an unshakeable certainty: we would face whatever came next, together. He felt like my anchor, my reason. He was my hero then, and he remains my hero today.

His arrival brought a sense of purpose and clarity that had been desperately missing. The overwhelming, primal love I felt for him gave me a strength I didn't know I possessed, a determination to navigate the daunting uncertainties of single parenthood and young adulthood. He became my guiding light, the tiny human who inspired me to try, finally, to be the best version of myself—for his sake. Through the exhausting blur of sleepless nights where the world seemed reduced to the dim glow of a nightlight and the rhythm of his breathing, the endless cycle of feedings and countless diapers, the fevers that brought worry lines to my brow and frantic calls to the pediatrician, the inevitable trials and tribulations of raising a child alone while barely scraping by financially, my love for him only grew stronger, deeper—a fierce, protective force.

Watching him grow and develop into his own unique person has been an incredible, humbling journey. From his first wobbly steps, arms outstretched for balance like a tiny tightrope walker, to his first tentative words, each milestone filled me with a profound pride and joy that eclipsed any personal achievement. He has taught me so much about resilience, about unconditional love, about the true meaning of family—not the one you're born into, necessarily, but the one you create and fiercely protect. He is not only my son, but also my teacher, my confidante, and my greatest source of inspiration.

After a few months of strained silence following my breaking off the engagement via that difficult email, Eric reached out again. His messages were tentative at first, hesitant, then filled with a growing desire to connect with Scott. He expressed remorse for his initial silence, acknowledging the hurt my email caused, and voiced a clear longing to be a part of his child's life.

As we corresponded cautiously—emails, occasional awkward phone calls where long pauses hung heavy, filled with unspoken questions—the sharp edges of resentment and the sting of my earlier rejection gradually gave way to a sense of hesitant understanding. Eric seemed genuinely invested in building a relationship with Scott, asking thoughtful questions about his development, expressing excitement over milestones like rolling over or grabbing toys. After several months of this tentative remote communication, Eric made a heartfelt plea: he offered to pay for a flight if I was willing to bring Scott to Philadelphia for a visit, for him to finally meet his son in person.

It was a difficult decision. The memory of why I'd ended the engagement, the feeling of fundamental unease, hadn't entirely faded. But the image of my son growing up without knowing his father, the potential guilt of denying that connection, felt wrong, too. Seeing Eric's apparent sincerity, his consistent effort over months, and perhaps still clinging to a sliver of hope for a conventional family structure, I saw the potential for healing—for Scott to have a relationship with his dad, and maybe even for growth for Eric and me. I agreed.

The visit to Philadelphia was a whirlwind of complex emotions. Stepping back into that city, into Eric's world, felt surreal. Seeing him interact with Scott for the first time was both heartwarming and unsettling. He was patient, kind, attentive—awkwardly but willingly changing diapers, attempting goofy faces to elicit smiles, rocking him gently when he fussed. He appeared the picture of a doting father. Watching them together in his apartment, seeing Scott respond to his father's voice, stirred feelings I thought were long buried. The familiar voice of doubt resurfaced, whispering insidious questions: *Perhaps this was the happy ending I was meant to have after all? Maybe I had been too hasty, too scared?*

Eric was a good man, fundamentally decent and kind. Seeing him with our son, witnessing his gentle care, made me question everything. I realized I still cared for him deeply, and I knew, despite everything, he cared for me. I even felt love for him—a comfortable, familiar, safe kind of love, like a worn-in sweater. But as time passed, as we navigated the complexities of co-parenting and eventually marriage, I would come to understand the profound, crucial difference between that comfortable love and being truly, deeply in love with someone.

Despite my lingering reservations, the vivid memory of why I'd ended the engagement just months before, the pull towards creating a traditional family unit for Scott was overwhelmingly strong. The societal pressure, the religious expectations I still hadn't fully shed, the desire to give my son the "normal" family I never truly had—it all conspired against my gut feeling, against the memory of that awkward proposal. We reconciled. And eventually, setting aside my unease, I rationalized it away and we married.

The day after my wedding, the supposed happiest day of my life, I found myself sitting in the living room of a close friend with a crushing weight of regret. Tears streamed down my face as I grappled with the immediate, visceral realization that I had made a grave mistake—repeating the feeling I'd had when I first accepted his proposal, only this time the commitment was legally binding. *What have I done?* The thought echoed. It felt too late to turn back. The vows had been spoken, the papers signed.

Despite the weight of my error, Scott and I moved back to Philadelphia to live with Eric as husband and wife. We would remain there for the next two years, attempting to build a life together. The distance from my family in Utah was a constant ache. The gray, damp winters felt heavy in a way I wasn't used to—more closed in, endlessly overcast. I missed the sharp, dry cold of Utah, the mountains silhouetted against the sky, the familiar faces at the grocery store, the easy camaraderie of my siblings, and my mom just a short drive away.

Homesickness gnawed at me. I began searching for job opportunities for Eric back in Utah, quietly networking and scouring listings. Eventually, perhaps seeing how deeply unhappy and isolated I was, he agreed to move back.

Shortly after settling into a new rental house in Utah, we learned I was pregnant again. Our second son, William, was born in 2005, followed by our youngest, Owen, in 2007. Our home quickly filled with the chaos and joy of three young boys.

I was fortunate to stay home with them in those early years. The days were demanding—endless diapers, picky eating battles, sticky fingerprints on every surface—but also full of small, grounding moments. The weight of a sleeping child on my shoulder, the sloppy kisses, the laughter in our living room—those things rooted me in a way nothing else had.

Motherhood had never been something I actively dreamed about. My younger self had chased romantic love, not children. But once I stepped into it, I found meaning and purpose I hadn't anticipated. My children became my world, and I was determined to give them the safety and unconditional love I hadn't always known.

I embraced the role fully—keeping our home warm and welcoming, baking cookies, connecting with neighborhood moms, planning playdates. But as the months passed, a quiet void began to take shape inside me. The comfort of routine couldn't hide the gnawing sense that something was missing—not from my role as a mother, but from me, and from my marriage.

I began to fill that emptiness with activity. Softball, volleyball, walking groups, coaching my sister's sports teams—anything to keep moving, to stay surrounded by noise and people. If I kept busy enough, I didn't have to acknowledge the growing distance between Eric and me, or the loneliness that settled in when the house was quiet. Years later, I would recognize this as a pattern I fell into after relationships ended or shifted—filling my calendar so full there was no room to feel the ache.

It took me a while to realize that my busyness was also a way to avoid time alone with him. We weren't friends in that deep, intimate way, and we were barely lovers.

Early in our relationship, I had been mid-sentence on a road trip when he interrupted me to point out something outside the window. When I said, "I was talking," he replied, "Oh, sorry, I didn't know." It wasn't malice—just disconnection. That pattern never really changed. Over the years, the emotional space between us grew into something unbridgeable.

At night, I'd edge myself to the far side of the bed. If he came in while I was awake, I'd pretend to sleep to avoid intimacy. The absence of touch—my primary love language—left me feeling unseen and unappreciated. His gifts and acts of service didn't meet my need for connection, and my inability then to recognize his gestures as love only deepened the divide.

We'd fight, things would improve briefly, then slide back into the same distance. Eventually, it became clear—we weren't growing together. We were coexisting, raising our boys, and drifting farther apart.

The realization was quiet at first, like a hairline crack in glass—barely visible, but spreading slowly. I didn't act on it right away. I buried myself in the routines of motherhood, community events, and anything that kept me moving forward without sitting too long in the truth.

But under the surface, another ache was growing—one that had nothing to do with Eric and everything to do with the parts of me that had never fully healed. Memories I tried to keep locked away would resurface at night when the house was still. Questions I'd never had the courage to ask began pressing harder, demanding answers. The busyness kept me from feeling it fully, but I knew the cracks were deepening.

I just didn't realize how close I was to breaking.

CHAPTER 15

(B)reaking

By 2010, the unresolved trauma from my childhood felt like a festering wound, often hidden beneath the surface of my busy life as a wife and mother, but always there, prone to infection. I found myself grappling with intense feelings of bitterness and resentment, not just towards my grandfather, but towards all the adults who had been present during those years of abuse. The questions cycled relentlessly in my mind, often late at night when the house was quiet: *How could they not see what was happening? Why didn't anyone step in to help me? Why did I always end up feeling like the bad one, constantly punished while he seemed to escape consequence?*

I tried looking at the situation from a parent's perspective, imagining how I would react if anything remotely similar happened to my own boys. The thought alone filled me with a visceral, protective rage, an overwhelming anxiety that made my chest tighten.

My brain felt flooded with unanswerable questions, each one further tormenting my already tortured soul. Despite the anger, I also felt incredible guilt for harboring these feelings towards people I loved— people who I knew had also been hurt and betrayed by my grandfather. The internal conflict was exhausting.

In a desperate attempt to bridge the gap between my pain and their understanding, I called my immediate family and asked them to come over. I wasn't seeking a confrontation; I wanted connection, validation, maybe even a shared path forward. I hoped that by opening up, we might begin to heal together.

When we gathered in the living room, I lay on the couch, tears streaming down my face, my body shaking as I tried to articulate the turmoil, the years of pent-up hurt and confusion. My father's gaze met mine—not with empathy or understanding, but with a hard, impatient expression. His words cut through my vulnerability like a blade: "Haven't we dealt with this shit already?"

The sting of his dismissal stopped my tears instantly. I watched helplessly as he stormed out, the door slamming behind him, his anger reverberating in the sudden, heavy silence. I had hoped my perspective as an adult, as a mother, might make him see me differently. Instead, the truth hit me hard—I was on my own in this part of my healing. Several family members preferred the comfort of silence, and I couldn't make them want to face what had happened.

The weight of that realization was suffocating. I knew that if I allowed my mental and emotional pain to take over completely, it would consume me. So I turned to the only thing I felt I could control—my body. I began a focused, determined weight loss journey. I threw myself into meal prep, calorie counting, and tracking every bite. Running became my sanctuary, a place where my mind could rest while my legs carried me forward. I believed that if I could master the physical, maybe—just maybe—it would give me the strength to one day face the mental.

Running soon turned into an obsession. I pounded the pavement mile after mile, chasing a version of myself that felt lighter, faster, more in control. Watching *The Biggest Loser* on television became a source of inspiration—seeing others transform their bodies fueled my own drive. I even applied to be on the show twice, imagining the radical, public transformation I might achieve. For the first time, I felt the sweet taste of sustained success in shedding the weight that had burdened me physically and symbolically for so long.

In 2011, another opportunity arose that further fueled my sense of purpose and served as a powerful distraction from the simmering marital discontent. My dad was finally realizing his lifelong dream of opening a large-scale, professional haunted house attraction. Despite the unresolved issues between us, I wholeheartedly dedicated myself to helping him, volunteering over forty hours each week. I sketched designs for scenes, built sets until my hands were raw, developed marketing strategies, recruited actors, and secured sponsorships from local businesses. Seeing the haunt come together was incredibly rewarding. The physical demands helped me continue my weight loss journey, and for a time, the shared project even seemed to strengthen my connection with my dad.

I was also actively trying to work on my marriage during this period, channeling my newfound energy into reconnecting with Eric, hoping the positive changes in other areas of my life might spill over. For a brief time, things felt hopeful. But the underlying issues in my marriage hadn't magically disappeared. Over the years, we found ourselves circling the same troubling theme: his persistent feelings of inadequacy, his dissatisfaction with his life, and his seeming inability to find contentment or take action to change things.

At first, I was his constant cheerleader—introducing him to friends, encouraging side businesses, affirming his value, supporting job changes. But as the years passed, my efforts waned. The emotional toll of trying to uplift someone unwilling or unable to take ownership of his own happiness became too heavy. Frustration and resentment replaced empathy.

The breaking point came when Eric, weary of caring for our three young boys in the evenings while I was at softball or the haunt, asked me to cut back. Although upset at feeling blamed, I reluctantly agreed—but I told him plainly that his happiness was his responsibility. If our family life wasn't enough for him, I said, it was okay to seek fulfillment elsewhere. Then I looked him in the eye and delivered the ultimatum I had long held back: "I swear to God, Eric, if we ever have this conversation again, I am leaving."

Months later, in September 2011, I had lost eighty pounds, felt more confident than ever, and accepted an invitation to a softball tournament in Florida. It was a taste of freedom—new friends, late-night laughter, and the unexpected attention of men, including Diego, whose concern for me after a concussion felt intoxicating. The night before we left, we kissed—nothing more, but enough to stir truths I could no longer ignore.

When I returned home, Eric's first words were a complaint about the boys' behavior while I was gone. The exact conversation I had sworn we would never have again unfolded almost immediately.

The bubble burst. Guilt from the kiss tangled with years of unmet needs and growing distance. Within days, I knew I was done.

One night after the haunt's opening weekend, I woke him and told him I was leaving. He begged, promised change, but my decision was final. A few days later, I told him about the kiss—not seeking forgiveness, but clearing the air. I knew, deep down, that the marriage had ended long before Florida. The kiss was just the catalyst.

It wasn't the kiss itself that ended the marriage—it was what it revealed. That moment was the catalyst because it forced me to face a truth I had been avoiding for years: I had never felt that kind of spark, that kind of pull, for the man I had married. We both deserved more than coexisting. We both deserved passion, connection, and a love that felt alive.

I realized I was teetering on the edge of becoming someone I never wanted to be—someone having affairs while carrying on in a marriage as if everything were fine. And in the quiet honesty of my own mind, I suspected Eric would never leave me, even if I crossed that line. That terrified me. I wanted a partner who would hold me accountable, who would inspire me to be my best self, and who would expect the same in return.

The kiss was not the betrayal that ended us—it was the mirror that showed me I had already left in every way that mattered.

CHAPTER 16

(F)allout

Going into the divorce, I was incredibly—perhaps willfully—naïve, especially regarding the financial fallout. My identity for the past eight years had revolved around being a stay-at-home mom, supplemented by fostering children and resale side hustles. I honestly assumed, with a startling lack of foresight, that life wouldn't change that drastically. I pictured the boys and me continuing to live in our house—the only home my youngest had ever known. I planned to keep fostering to bring in some income and supplement that with a part-time job. In my simplistic calculations, I believed Eric's child support combined with my earnings would be enough for us to manage, to maintain a semblance of our previous life.

However, that fragile illusion shattered abruptly when Eric informed me that he intended to keep the house. The words hit me like a physical blow. Suddenly, the floor dropped out from under my assumptions. I had nowhere to go, no savings to speak of, and three young children depending on me. Panic set in as I was forced to drastically rethink our entire situation. A quick, terrifying assessment of apartment rental costs versus my earning potential made it painfully clear: I would need to work at least two jobs, maybe more, just to afford even a basic, cramped apartment for myself and the boys. The dream of maintaining stability dissolved into the stark reality of survival.

Despite the shock and fear, I had no desire to involve lawyers or engage in a protracted, bitter fight with Eric over assets. Our separation, while painful and stemming from years of disconnect, wasn't fueled by deep animosity at that specific moment; it felt more like a sad, inevitable conclusion. I still believed, perhaps foolishly, that we could reach a fair agreement regarding custody and other necessary arrangements amicably, without legal battles draining our already limited resources. In that spirit of wanting a clean break, I didn't ask for alimony—something I likely would have been entitled to—and I gave him our home outright. I left with virtually no money but half the debt we had accumulated, taking only what was necessary: some furniture, my clothes, a few of the boys' belongings, and the most sentimental items I could fit into boxes. I didn't need much. I wanted freedom more than things.

When we initially calculated child support, the arrangement reflected my desperate reality at that moment: I was working two demanding, low-wage jobs, juggling shifts that often stretched late into the night or started before dawn. This meant Eric inevitably had majority custody simply due to my grueling schedule. As a result, the official child support amount was set shockingly low—less than $100 per month—an amount that barely covered a week's worth of groceries, let alone rent or utilities.

The strain of working those two jobs took its toll almost immediately. I was constantly exhausted, running on fumes and Diet Pepsi. My time with the boys felt rushed and stressed. I found myself burning out within just a few months, sinking deeper into debt as unexpected expenses cropped up and paychecks failed to stretch far enough. Struggling desperately to pay rent on our apartment felt like a constant battle against a rising tide. Then came the humiliating blow of having my car repossessed—the first car I had ever financed by myself, my only reliable transportation—adding another layer of difficulty and shame to my already precarious situation. How could I get to two jobs without a car? How could I get the boys to school? Panic flared again.

I began selling more of my belongings online—furniture, electronics, keepsakes I had treasured—keeping only the absolute essentials: my clothes, the boys' necessities, and a few irreplaceable sentimental items. The apartment felt emptier and emptier.

For the first few years after the divorce, my income rarely exceeded $15 an hour, often dipping as low as $9 an hour at one point. Combined with my lifelong struggle of managing money, there were many terrifying days when I genuinely didn't know how I would feed my family. Ramen noodles, cheap boxed macaroni and cheese, peanut butter sandwiches—these became staples. The constant financial stress, the feeling of never quite having enough, was a heavy weight. The reality of single motherhood, especially after years of relative financial security within marriage, hit me like a physical blow, leaving me feeling inadequate and perpetually anxious.

After the initial burnout phase, realizing the two-job grind was unsustainable and detrimental to my time with the boys, I managed to transition back to one full-time job. This shift, while reducing my income further, allowed me to pursue equal custody of my children. It wasn't an easy process—it required time, patience, navigating paperwork, and likely some difficult conversations filled with tension and old resentments. But eventually, Eric agreed to a verbal 50/50 custody arrangement. Seeing my boys more consistently, having them half the time, felt like a monumental victory—a crucial step toward rebuilding my life and strengthening my role as their mother.

Despite this positive step forward in terms of shared parenting time, child support remained a persistent, contentious issue. My income had decreased significantly from the two-job period when the initial order was set, and I was now spending significantly more time (and therefore resources) caring for the boys, yet it would be years before the child support payments were formally adjusted through the courts to align with the actual custody arrangement and my reduced income. While the financial aspect was undoubtedly frustrating, creating immense and ongoing stress, it was not my primary focus or the main source of pain regarding the divorce itself. The emotional toll of the conflict was far worse.

Initially, Eric and I managed to communicate relatively effectively regarding the boys' schedules and basic needs. We navigated the logistics of co-parenting with a semblance of civility, perhaps both wanting to minimize conflict for the children's sake. However, the dynamics shifted dramatically, becoming significantly more hostile, when he entered a serious relationship with Cindy. Disagreements became commonplace, escalating quickly. Pick-up and drop-off times became points of contention. Differences in discipline or household rules led to arguments. Nearly every interaction seemed to devolve into conflict, laced with accusations or passive aggression. The fragile peace we had established disintegrated, replaced by a constant state of tension.

There was a brief period where Eric, perhaps recognizing the financial disparity, agreed to voluntarily increase child support payments to match the amount calculated by the state's online calculator. This offered a glimmer of hope, a potential easing of the constant financial pressure. However, this progress was short-lived. Soon after, I lost my job unexpectedly and was therefore available during the upcoming fall break to care for the boys while they were out of school. Eric and Cindy had planned for her to watch them. I argued—logically, I thought—that it made no sense for the boys to stay with his girlfriend when I, their mother, was readily available and wanted them.

The argument escalated. Whether in direct retaliation for this disagreement or due to other factors influenced by his new relationship, my subsequent child support check reverted to the meager amount stipulated in our original decree, rather than the increased amount we had verbally agreed upon just weeks before.

This pattern of arguments, financial manipulation, and co-parenting frustrations persisted for several years, creating a tumultuous and emotionally draining post-divorce reality. It often felt like they were actively trying to keep my children from me, using visitation schedules or excuses to limit my time, while simultaneously manipulating child support payments, pushing me emotionally and financially to the brink. Cindy, in particular, seemed to insert herself into situations unnecessarily, escalating conflict rather than easing it.

I vividly remember an incident where she appeared at my son's school one day when Eric and I were having a disagreement about me spending a few extra minutes with Owen after class. I was simply sitting with Owen on a patch of grass near my car, still on school property, talking about his day, when Cindy materialized, standing just a few yards away, her phone pointed directly at us, recording our every move. There was no reason for her to be there, no reason to record a simple mother-son conversation. The intrusion felt deliberate, calculated, designed to intimidate and document, turning a simple moment into evidence for some future conflict.

It further escalated the tension between Eric and me, making co-parenting feel less like a partnership and more like navigating a hostile minefield. Looking back, I accept my share of blame for the toxicity of this period. I was often immature and mean in my responses, retorting with name-calling and allowing myself to get immersed in a level of drama I had never expected or experienced before. It was exhausting and damaging for everyone involved, especially the children caught in the middle. In hindsight, it's clear I was deep in crisis during this time, reacting from a place of hurt, fear, and instability rather than thoughtful consideration.

Looking back, I can see that this wasn't just the fallout of a divorce—it was the unravelling of the life I had built, piece by piece. Financially, I was barely hanging on. Emotionally, I was raw, reactive, and constantly on edge. My sense of stability had been stripped away, and in its place was a gnawing emptiness I didn't yet know how to fill.

That emptiness—and my desperation to escape it—would soon lead me into another kind of storm.

CHAPTER 17

(A)drift

The years after my divorce felt like being caught in a rip current—no matter how hard I kicked, I couldn't get back to shore. I was in constant motion, moving apartments, moving my boys between households, moving from one job to another, but never moving toward stability. I told myself it was survival, but looking back, I was running—sometimes sprinting—away from stillness.

Stillness meant feeling. And I didn't want to feel.

Dating and going out became my main distraction, my primary focus, and a sharp double-edged sword. I threw myself into it with the same energy some people pour into a career. It was as if I had been handed a second chance at the college years I never had—years I'd skipped entirely in my twenties when I was busy getting married, raising babies, and trying to live up to the role of "good girl." Now, in my thirties, I was making up for lost time.

There were so many firsts—my first one-night stand, my first kiss in a bar, my first late-night stumbling home in heels, my first time traveling somewhere on a whim with someone I barely knew. These weren't just new experiences; they were acts of rebellion. After years of doing everything "right" and still never being enough for my father to love me or help me heal, I decided I might as well stop trying to please anyone.

That's when she appeared—Freya. Goddess of love and war. The part of me that was bold, unapologetic, and untouchable. Freya didn't second-guess. Freya didn't care what people thought. She took up space, demanded attention, and chased pleasure with both hands open. When the world saw her, they didn't see the woman weighed down by bills, custody exchanges, and empty cupboards—they saw confidence, energy, and allure. Freya was my armor.

I wasn't aware of it then, but the patterns were already written deep inside me. I chased validation like oxygen—through attention, through busyness, through anything that made me feel chosen, even temporarily. It didn't matter if it was healthy. It didn't matter if it was safe. If someone showed me interest, I mistook it for worth. If someone pulled away, I mistook it for a challenge.

I moved often—sometimes into my own apartments, sometimes with roommates, and more than once back into my parents' or siblings' homes. Every place was temporary, like I was waiting for my real life to start. The sound of packing tape peeling off the roll became as familiar as my own heartbeat. Cardboard boxes sat half-unpacked in corners, their flaps sagging open, a constant reminder that I was only passing through.

The chaos outside matched the chaos inside. I was working whatever jobs I could find, juggling hours that left me eating dinner in my car or collapsing into bed long after midnight. Some months, the fridge held little more than milk, bread, and whatever was on sale. My parenting during this time was a patchwork of love and absence. I adored my boys, but I wasn't present in the way they needed. Too often, they got the exhausted, distracted version of me—the one counting down minutes until bedtime, not because I didn't want to be with them, but because I didn't know how to be with myself.

Anxiety was a constant hum beneath everything. Rent due dates loomed like storm clouds. Unexpected bills felt like waves knocking me under, leaving me coughing and scrambling to breathe. I was in survival mode, but the problem with living that way is you never stop to ask what you're surviving *for*.

Underneath it all, the unhealed parts of me were steering the ship. I didn't recognize it then, but the choices I made were a direct extension of wounds I hadn't addressed. I was searching for safety in all the wrong places, running from the kind of accountability and stillness that might have forced me to look at my own pain.

I didn't know it yet, but the breaking point was coming. And when it did, I would finally have to face the truth I'd been outrunning.

CHAPTER 18

(V)iolation

O nline dating, as I've mentioned, was a double-edged sword. On one hand, it was incredibly exciting to connect with so many new people, and I was fortunate enough to form some deep and lasting friendships with people I met online. These friends became my rocks, offering unwavering support and helping me through some incredibly difficult times. They were always there to pick me up, dust me off, and remind me of my strength.

On the other hand, the anonymity and vastness of the online world also exposed me to some truly dark and dangerous individuals. I encountered more than my fair share of creeps and predators, and I was subjected to a range of horrific experiences, from financial exploitation and theft to a kidnapping incident by a friend and her boyfriend, and eventually, assault. Looking back, I'm still amazed that I survived it all. It's a testament to my resilience and the support of my loved ones that I'm still here to share my story.

In November 2013, adrift in this personal storm, I hit what felt like the lowest point of my life, a new rock bottom that redefined despair.

I met Andrew on a dating site, one notorious for its lack of barriers – anyone can message anyone without needing to match first. He was older than me, presenting himself in his profile as a successful, put-together financial advisor. His pictures were passable, but something felt slightly off. I wasn't physically attracted to him, a fact I stated honestly upfront when he messaged me, hoping to deter him gently. "You're not really my type," I replied, "but thanks."

Despite this clear statement, he persisted, smoothly pivoting to claim he was more interested in friendship than a romantic relationship anyway. After some back-and-forth messaging, his persistence wearing down my already weak boundaries – maybe just being friends wouldn't hurt? – I cautiously gave him my phone number.

Initially, the text conversations were harmless enough, just typical getting-to-know-you chatter about work, hobbies, and the weather. Then, one night, out of the blue, he sent me a picture of himself dressed head-to-toe in women's clothing. I stared at the picture, completely taken aback, a wave of confusion and discomfort washing over me. I didn't respond immediately. He later texted an explanation, claiming it was just an old Halloween costume, that he was just joking around. But I couldn't shake the feeling that it wasn't a joke, that he'd sent it deliberately to test my reaction, to gauge my boundaries, to see how far he could push. I felt guilty for judging him – maybe it was just a joke? – but also increasingly uneasy. My intuition, that quiet inner voice I so often ignored, was whispering caution. I let the conversation fade, and stopped responding to his messages.

A few months later, after deleting and recreating my profile on the dating site (a common tactic in my chaotic dating life, hoping for a fresh start), he messaged me again, instantly recognizing my new profile. He was skilled at manipulation, knowing exactly how to make me feel guilty for having ghosted him, playing on my insecurities. Once more, he asked if we could go out. I reiterated, firmly this time, that I wasn't interested in dating him. He insisted again, smoothly, "We can just be friends. No pressure."

The chilly late fall air hinted at the excitement of basketball season, and the Utah Jazz were playing a much-anticipated game that evening. My initial plan was to find company at a local sports bar, wanting the camaraderie, the shared thrill of the game. After reaching out to several friends without success, loneliness creeping in, the familiar dread of spending another night alone settling upon me, I made the fateful decision to text Andrew. *Maybe just as friends? Just to watch the game?*

He responded enthusiastically, almost too quickly. He expressed his desire to meet up but mentioned he had already invited friends over to his house to watch the game. He extended an invitation for me to join them. I initially declined, the thought of going to his house feeling wrong, unsafe. My intuition screamed caution again. But Andrew persisted, painting a picture of a fun, casual evening – barbecued bratwursts, good company, friendly sports banter. He asked if I could stop at the liquor store on my way to pick up some specific items he needed for drinks. Despite my deep reluctance about going to his house, despite the nagging sense of unease that coiled in my stomach, the fear of loneliness, the pressure of not wanting to disappoint him (a stranger!), and the fear of being seen as flaky or judgmental overshadowed my intuition. Against my better judgment, ignoring the blaring internal warning signs, I agreed, stopped at the liquor store, and went to Andrew's house.

As I pulled into his quiet suburban driveway, a fresh wave of unease washed over me. The absence of other cars was striking; where were the friends' cars? I had expected a small gathering, maybe two or three other vehicles lining the street. My mind raced, grasping for explanations. Perhaps his friends lived nearby, just a short walk away. Maybe they carpooled. I clung to these flimsy hopes, a desperate attempt to quell the rising disquiet, the feeling that I was walking into a trap.

When Andrew opened the front door, my breath hitched. He looked nothing like his profile picture, which must have been years, maybe decades, old. Time had etched deep lines onto his face, his frame was gaunt beneath the oversized track jacket he wore, emphasizing his frailty. He looked tired, worn, and significantly older. A wave of disappointment crashed over me – another deception, another red flag.

I never felt comfortable. My Spidey senses were on high alert from the start. When he hugged me, the goosebumps on my skin weren't from chemistry—they were from something deeper. His greeting was warm—too warm—and overly enthusiastic. He pulled me into an embrace that lingered just a second too long, not in a way that comforted me, but in a way that unsettled me. It didn't feel like connection—it felt like manipulation dressed as kindness.

Inside, the sight of the unopened bratwurst package sitting forlornly on the kitchen counter jolted me back to reality. A cold shiver ran down my spine. Where were the friends? Where was the BBQ he'd mentioned? A primal instinct urged me to turn around, make an excuse, and flee. *Just leave!* But I was frozen, trapped by politeness, by fear, by the horrifying realization that I was alone in this stranger's house, a nightmare rapidly unfolding. His flimsy excuse about his friends canceling at the very last minute only amplified my fear, confirming the lie.

The living room felt claustrophobic, the air thick with an unspoken, predatory tension. He offered me a drink, using the mixers and alcohol I had brought. I watched him make the first one, something fruity from a pitcher he combined with liquor. One drink, maybe two sips, was all it took for my head to start spinning, my tolerance low, my body already flooded with stress hormones. Andrew insisted I have another, taking my glass back to the kitchen to refill it while I stayed rooted on the worn fabric of the couch, paralyzed by a growing sense of dread. I didn't watch him make the second drink. When he returned, my mind was already screaming warnings. The room seemed to tilt, my vision blurring at the edges, sounds becoming muffled. His voice seemed to echo from a distance as he urged me to drink more, talking about the game, his words barely registering. Soon, he was gently urging me up, leading me towards the bedroom, his hand too firm on my arm, and I felt utterly powerless to resist, my body heavy and unresponsive, refusing to cooperate with my mind's desperate commands to escape. *No, no, no...*

Panic surged through me, a terrifying, paralyzing wave. My mind raced, screaming, *Get out! Run! Fight!* But my body betrayed me. It felt heavy, disconnected, unresponsive. I was trapped in a horrifying paradox – mentally fighting, physically frozen. It was tonic immobility, though I wouldn't have the words for it for years. In the midst of the internal chaos, the terror, a chilling, pragmatic thought emerged, a detached survival mechanism kicking in: *Endure this, just endure this, and it will be over. You never have to see him again. Just survive.*

I vaguely recall getting undressed, the memory hazy, fragmented, dreamlike, as if watching myself from a distance. Over the course of what felt like several hours, though my sense of time was completely distorted, I drifted in and out of consciousness. At one point, I awoke to the horrifying sensation of cold, hard objects being inserted into various parts of my body, a violation that felt both surreal and deeply degrading. Another time, I surfaced briefly, my head lolling, to find Andrew holding me up from behind, waving pungent smelling salts under my nose, trying to rouse me from the stupor he had likely induced.

The disorientation was overwhelming. Later, I found myself somehow in the bathroom, the cool, smooth tile against my bare skin a stark contrast to the hazy confusion clouding my mind. My reflection in the mirror looked alien, eyes wide and unfocused. My eyes darted around the unfamiliar room – beige towels, a cluttered counter – desperately seeking something, anything, familiar to ground me in the terrifying disorientation. *Escape.* The thought pulsed weakly through the fog. *I need to escape.*

Time seemed to warp and stretch, marked only by hazy moments of terrifying awareness followed by periods of blankness. What felt like hours later, maybe early morning, a sliver of lucidity returned, enough for me to realize I absolutely had to leave, to get out of that house. But as I tried to gather my scattered clothes, he wanted me to stay. He spoke of cuddling, of making breakfast together, his words painting a picture of a tender, romantic night, a reality completely, horrifyingly alien to the fragmented, terrifying memories swimming in my head. The dissonance between his casual intimacy and my own internal landscape of violation sent a fresh chill down my spine.

I declined his offer, my voice barely a whisper, raspy and weak. "I need to get to work", I managed, the lie tasting like ash in my mouth. His response was eerily calm, detached, almost cheerful, a chilling contrast to the turmoil raging within me. "Okay", he said easily. "Have a good day. Call me as soon as you get home so I know you're safe." The words, the implied possession, the utter disregard for what had actually happened, hung in the air, heavy with unspoken threat.

The drive home was a blur, a hazy, disorienting journey through streets that seemed unfamiliar, my hands shaking on the steering wheel, my body trembling. I navigated on autopilot, pulling into the parking lot of my small apartment building with a sense of profound relief mixed with deep dread. I could barely remember the physical act of getting out of the car, fumbling with my keys, stumbling into my apartment, and collapsing into bed, fully clothed. My mind reeled, trying to piece together the fragmented horror, the gaps in time. A relentless barrage of questions echoed in the suffocating silence of my bedroom: *How had I allowed myself to reach this point? Why did I ignore my intuition? Why did I feel so powerless, so utterly incapable of standing up for myself? What was fundamentally wrong with me that I couldn't escape this cycle of self-destructive behavior and dangerous situations?* The self-blame was immediate, intense, overwhelming.

The insistent buzz of my phone on the nightstand cut through the silence like a physical blow. A text from Andrew. "Did you make it home okay?" followed quickly by another: "Had a great time last night. Really enjoyed our evening together. Looking forward to seeing you again soon." A wave of nausea washed over me, bile rising in my throat. *Who was this man?* This delusional stranger who seemed to have fabricated an entirely different reality in his mind? The disparity between his perception of the evening and my own traumatic experience was bewildering, terrifying, and deeply disturbing.

The texts continued to arrive throughout the day, each notification a jarring reminder of the gaping hole between his imagined relationship and the grim reality I had endured. He asked when we could meet again. He boasted of telling his friends about me (the friends who supposedly canceled?). He extended an invitation to join his group for a tailgating party at an upcoming football game. With each message, my sense of dread, despair, and violation intensified. I felt trapped, suffocating under the weight of his relentless pursuit and the haunting realization that I had once again become entangled in a web of manipulation, deceit, and profound violation.

When I finally found the courage, hours later, fueled by a growing sense of outrage beneath the fear, to respond, telling him his behavior was completely inappropriate and deranged, that what happened was not okay, he feigned shock and disbelief. He claimed he was truly sorry if I felt uncomfortable, insisting that if I had expressed discomfort at any point, he would have immediately stopped – a classic, infuriating gaslighting tactic. Despite his empty apologies, I firmly told him to cease all contact. My plea fell on deaf ears. He continued to reach out, his persistence feeling like another form of violation.

Hours later, still reeling, numb, a close friend texted, a simple "How was your night?" Unable to contain the trauma any longer, the dam finally broke. I called him. The story poured out between ragged sobs, recounting the fragmented events, the fear, the confusion, the violation. He listened patiently, his voice calm and steady on the other end of the line. Then, he firmly told me what I couldn't yet fully grasp: "Amber, you need to call the police." I hesitated, overwhelmed with shame and self-blame. *I went there. I drank. I didn't fight hard enough.* The old tapes played relentlessly. Even though I hadn't truly wanted it, hadn't truly consented in any meaningful way, the complexities, the gray areas I perceived, felt paralyzing. My friend was unwavering. "What you described was not consensual sex. That was rape."

Still grappling with fear and uncertainty, the word *rape* echoing terrifyingly in my mind, I called my sister and confided in her, my voice trembling. I told her what happened and that I was being urged to contact the police. The thought terrified me. The justice system had failed me miserably as a child, an innocent child who had done nothing wrong. *If they weren't willing to protect me then, why would they protect me now, after my own questionable choices led me to his door? They'll blame me,* I thought. But then my thoughts shifted, momentarily, away from myself, towards other potential victims. His behavior felt predatory, calculated, practiced. I was certain this wasn't the first time he had acted this way. If I didn't speak up, it wouldn't be the last. My sister listened, horrified, and agreed. "You have to report it, Amber."

I reached out to one more friend, Mike, who lived nearby. Thankfully, he came over right away, his calm, reassuring presence a much-needed anchor in the storm. He sat with me, listened again, offered quiet support as I made the difficult, terrifying call to the police, my hand shaking as I dialed, my voice barely a whisper as I explained why I was calling. He stayed with me as the uniformed officers arrived, their presence filling my small living room, and as they took my initial report. The officers, however, maintained a detached, impersonal demeanor throughout. Their questions felt routine, scripted, their expressions neutral, clinical. It felt as if they didn't believe me, or perhaps felt no empathy, simply going through the necessary motions because it was their job. Their lack of warmth, their professional distance, only added to my distress and feelings of isolation, making me feel like a case number rather than a victim of a violent crime.

As part of their procedure, they asked me to go to the hospital for a rape exam. The request triggered an immediate, visceral flood of unwanted memories – vivid images of being eight years old, small and terrified in a cold hospital room, undergoing a similar invasive examination after disclosing the abuse by my grandfather. Anxiety and fear washed over me, making it hard to breathe. The thought of reliving that experience, the probing questions, the collection of evidence, the feeling of my body being treated like a crime scene again, felt almost unbearable.

Could I go through this again? Did I have the strength?

Mike drove me to the hospital and stayed with me the entire time, waiting patiently in the stark waiting room, a silent, supportive presence in the sterile, impersonal environment. The exam itself was as difficult as I had feared, a necessary violation in the pursuit of potential justice. The exam eventually concluded that there were internal injuries consistent with force, but the report carried the devastatingly ambiguous note that such trauma could occur during consensual sex — a line that landed like yet another blow. Another loophole. Another way to question what I knew in my body to be true. I had given blood and urine samples, hoping for proof of drugging, but the results of the toxicology report would take months to come back, leaving me suspended in a state of agonizing uncertainty.

Meanwhile, armed with a search warrant based on my statement, detectives meticulously combed through Andrew's residence. They discovered items – perhaps specific objects I mentioned being used during the assault, or evidence corroborating my timeline – that provided additional support for parts of my statement. Despite this mounting physical evidence, Andrew remained steadfast in his denial when questioned, vehemently rejecting the rape accusation and insisting that all sexual activity had been entirely consensual, that I had been a willing participant. His lies felt like another assault.

A few days before Thanksgiving, the ordeal took another sinister turn. I received a long, deeply upsetting text message from Andrew. He wrote about the painful anniversary of his daughter's tragic death by suicide years prior, attempting to create a false sense of shared grief, claiming he understood the pain I would feel being without my kids (referencing my custody situation). Then came the chilling threat: if I didn't drop my case against him, he would hire the best lawyers money could buy to ensure I lost my ongoing custody battle with Eric. I was shocked and terrified – I had never mentioned my custody case to him. *How did he know? Had he been investigating me?* The calculated cruelty, using his dead daughter and my children as weapons, was horrifying. I immediately contacted the detective handling my case, forwarding the message. The detective warned Andrew that any further contact would result in a restraining order. That was the last time I heard from him, but the threat lingered, a testament to his willingness to intimidate, manipulate, and control.

In late December, the final blow came via a phone call from the District Attorney's office. The toxicology report had come back negative. There was no scientific proof I had been drugged. With a somber, apologetic tone, the DA explained that without more substantial evidence – without the definitive proof of drugging to counter the lack of clear physical resistance – they would not be filing charges. The news was crushing, devastating. It felt like the justice system had failed me once again, leaving me violated, traumatized, unheard, and without any sense of closure or retribution. He would face no consequences.

The experience was shattering. While deeply grateful for the small circle of people who rallied around me, offering unwavering support, believing me without question, I was also consumed by anger. Anger at myself, primarily, for putting myself in that situation, for ignoring my intuition, for not fighting harder. But also a deep, simmering anger at the friends and family who remained silent, who offered platitudes but no real support, whose silence felt like a tacit agreement that I had somehow deserved it, or that it was too messy, too uncomfortable to engage with. A part of me believed they thought I deserved it—my dad, maybe a few others in the family. My dad has never said a word. Not then, not ever. And in a world that so often points fingers at victims, their silence sounded like agreement. Like judgment in disguise. This was another moment in my life when I needed a protector. But instead of safety, I got distance. And whether it was avoidance, disbelief, or something worse, I was left alone with the shame they wouldn't carry — but wouldn't help me put down, either.

The week that followed the assault was a blur of profound pain and despair. I felt like a mere shadow of myself, haunted by the trauma, by the injustice, by the feeling of being utterly broken. Sleep offered no escape, even with the aid of Ambien, prescribed by a doctor and taken for the first time in my life in a desperate attempt to find respite from the relentless anguish, the replays of the night, the crushing weight of it all. My mother graciously cared for my boys on my scheduled days, her quiet presence a balm, recognizing I was in no condition to provide them with the care and attention they needed. My focus narrowed solely to survival, to simply getting through each agonizing day, one breath at a time. Beyond the immediate grief and anger, this violation left a deeper, more insidious scar, fundamentally altering my physical responses. This was one of the moments that altered something in me.

The trauma Andrew inflicted—layered on top of the earlier abuse by my grandfather—rewired my body's sense of safety. My nervous system learned to sound the alarm at the sight of men who resembled those who had harmed me. It wasn't attraction I lost—it was access to safety in my own body.

From that point on, I experienced a full-body warning when faced with men who shared their physical traits: a tremor, a tightening, a visceral recoil at the thought of being touched.

For me, it wasn't about race—it was about pattern recognition burned into my survival wiring. The ones who crossed every boundary, who made my body unsafe, all looked the same to me.

It wasn't just Andrew. It was my own father. It was men in the church. It was officers and judges and therapists who held authority but not compassion. It was the men who silenced me, dismissed me, controlled me, or watched me suffer and did nothing.

This wasn't a choice. It was a trauma response—a survival mechanism many victims of child sexual abuse know too well. For some, the recoil is from a gender. For others, it's from a certain look, voice, or scent. Trauma imprints these associations deep in the brain's implicit memory, triggering the body's defense systems long before conscious thought can intervene.

My body thought it was keeping me safe, but it also kept me isolated. Another wall between me and the life I wanted. Between me and connection. Between me and healing.

CHAPTER 19

(A)rrest

fter that initial week lost in a fog of pain, despair, and medicated sleep, the sharp ache of missing my boys began to cut through the numbness. The yearning to see them, to hold them, became unbearable—a physical need almost as strong as breathing. The absence of their small bodies, their specific smells, their chaotic energy, felt like a phantom limb. I longed for their comforting hugs, their innocent laughter, the grounding presence that reminded me there was still good in the world, that I still had a reason to fight.

I had chosen not to tell Eric about the assault; the state of our co-parenting relationship made him the furthest person from whom I wanted support or solace. Revealing such vulnerability felt impossible, unsafe. He was aware, however, that my mother had been caring for the boys during my scheduled time over the past week and had expressed his displeasure, likely viewing it as another failure on my part, another inconvenience.

Complicating matters, Eric's girlfriend, Cindy, and her children had recently moved into his home. This transition was proving difficult for our sons, Scott, William, and Owen. They were struggling to adjust to the new family dynamic, the sudden presence of new people in their space, the shifting rules and expectations. As a result, Eric, Cindy, her children, and our boys were all attending therapy sessions together, ostensibly to address the friction.

They had scheduled one such therapy session for a day that, according to our custody arrangement, I was legally entitled to have the boys. However, we had made a verbal agreement to swap days so they could attend. An invitation was extended for me to attend with them, likely in hopes of working through some of the overall issues and escalating co-parenting conflicts.

On the morning of the session, however, still reeling from the trauma of the previous week, the thought of sitting in a sterile therapy room, dissecting family dynamics under fluorescent lights, felt utterly impossible. My emotional skin felt raw, exposed. I made the decision to cancel my attendance. Concurrently, the ache to see my children intensified into a desperate need. I expressed this strong desire to Eric, needing their presence more than ever. This upset him, as I had previously agreed to give up my allotted days earlier that week for the therapy arrangement. He voiced his frustration, accusing me of changing the schedule again, of being unreliable. He mentioned his intention to return to work after the therapy session. I countered, my own voice likely rising, fueled by pain and lack of sleep, that it was illogical for the boys to spend time with his girlfriend if I, their mother, was available and desperately needed to see them.

In response to my concerns, or perhaps just to end the argument, Eric decided he would stay home after therapy but promised to call me if he changed his mind and decided to go back to work. The promise felt flimsy, unreliable.

Eric lived close to my parents, and I would often pass his house on my way to theirs. As I drove that day, heading towards my parents' house after canceling the therapy session, anger and resentment churned within me. Anger at Eric, at Cindy, at the situation, at the universe. Anger fueled by the recent assault, the feeling of powerlessness, the injustice of my current circumstances. I had no conscious intention of stopping at his house; I just wanted to drive by, maybe offer a silent, bitter middle finger to the house that held so many complicated, painful memories of our failed marriage. The mere sight of the familiar brick facade fueled my bitterness.

But as I approached, my heart pounding with a toxic mix of grief, rage, and exhaustion, I noticed Eric outside in the driveway with Cindy's young son. They were both getting into his car. I assumed he was heading back to work, breaking his promise, leaving the boys with her when I was available, when I needed them.

In a blinding flash of rage, all rational thought, all self-preservation, evaporated. It felt like a switch flipped, plunging me into red-hot fury. I disregarded my better judgment, the little voice screaming *No!*, and slammed on the brakes, the tires screeching loudly on the quiet suburban street. Regret washed over me instantly, cold and sharp even amidst the heat of my anger—I shouldn't have stopped. But it was too late. My anger, raw, unprocessed, fueled by trauma and desperation, had taken complete control. Seeing red, I threw the car door open and stomped up the driveway, my heavy footsteps echoing my fury on the concrete.

Eric met me at the garage, his expression shifting from surprise to alarm, attempting to halt my advance with outstretched hands. "I want my kids!" I roared, my voice hoarse, laced with a desperation that bordered on hysteria. "Stop keeping my kids from me!"

Cindy stood just inside the garage, partially obscured by shadows, a silent, perhaps smug, observer to the escalating conflict.

Undeterred, fueled by the singular, primal need to see my children, to hold them, I pressed on toward the garage door leading into the house. Eric positioned himself between me and the entrance, his hands up, pleading, "Amber, calm down! Just calm down, I'll get them."

As he opened the interior door and called for the boys, their names echoing strangely in the tense air, Cindy's shrill voice cut through like shattered glass. "It's not your day to see them," she declared, stepping forward into the light, her expression hard. "You need to leave."

Her words, her audacity, ignited a fresh wave of fury within me. Eric had just summoned my children—who was she to dictate when I could see them? Her physical proximity felt suffocating; I could smell the faint scent of her perfume mixed with something else, maybe her breath, on my face. In that moment, overwhelmed, provoked, feeling cornered, I shoved her away—a reactive, impulsive push that caused her to stumble into Eric. Chaos erupted instantly.

Cindy shrieked, barking orders at her son to call the police. Hearing the commotion, I could now hear my boys crying from inside the house. My focus shifted instantly. Forgetting any thought of leaving the property, my only instinct was to get to them. I turned towards the front door of the house. But as I turned, Eric's forceful shove from behind sent me sprawling, hard, onto the unforgiving concrete driveway. The shock of his physical attack momentarily stunned me. I sat there for a few seconds, the rough concrete biting into my skin, the world tilting, trying to process what had just happened, before survival instinct, sheer adrenaline, kicked in. I leaped to my feet and sprinted towards the front door of the house, desperate to reach my children.

I burst inside just before Eric could lock me out, his attempts to block me from reaching the kitchen futile. The scene that greeted me sent another wave of shock and horror through me. My eldest son, Scott, sat frozen at the kitchen table, his eyes wide with fear. Cindy stood over him, her phone shoved inches from his face, recording the entire chaotic scene, her voice sharp and commanding. Scott's tearful pleas, "Stop it! Please stop!" echoed in the suddenly too-small kitchen, tearing at my already shredded heart.

William came charging up the stairs then, alerted by the shouting, his small face crumpled in distress, his cries filling the air. He attempted to flee through the garage, perhaps seeking escape from the terrifying adult drama, but Cindy, quick and sharp, grabbed his arm, preventing his escape. He twisted free, wrenching his arm away, and ran straight to me, burying his face in my legs. Owen followed close behind, his eyes wide, clinging to me. With all the boys sobbing, clinging tightly to me, their small bodies trembling, we bolted back outside into the harsh afternoon light.

Knowing the police were undoubtedly on their way, sirens likely already wailing in the distance, we sought refuge across the street, huddling together on a neighbor's perfectly manicured lawn. We waited, the four of us trembling, our combined sobs mingling with the rising fear and sickening uncertainty of what was to come. The flashing red and blue lights reflecting off the houses seemed inevitable now, a harbinger of doom.

The scene unfolded before me like a chaotic, slow-motion blur— the arrival of police cars, the stern faces of the officers, the neighbors peering from behind curtains. It was a maelstrom of emotions and actions that I never, in my wildest nightmares, anticipated would culminate in my own arrest. I knew I shouldn't have been there. I knew creating a scene, losing control like that, was wrong. But never, not even for a fleeting moment, had the thought crossed my mind that I, the mother trying to see her children, the recent victim of a violent crime, could be the one arrested.

The officer's questions came sharp and fast, his tone clipped, impersonal. "What happened here?" "Did you push her?" "Why did you enter the house?" It didn't take long, feeling the weight of the officers' dispassionate scrutiny, for the gravity of the situation to sink in with horrifying clarity. My world tilted violently on its axis as I realized I was in serious trouble. The request for a lawyer slipped from my lips, a desperate grasp for some kind of protection. It was met not with understanding, but with the chilling command that ripped through the fog of my disbelief: "Turn around. Put your hands behind your back."

The cold steel of the handcuffs clicked shut around my wrists, biting into my skin. The officer recited my Miranda rights, his voice a monotonous drone against the frantic pounding in my ears. I stood there, numb, my mind reeling, unable to process the reality. *Arrested? Me? For this?*

As they led me toward the waiting patrol car, the heavy thud of the door closing behind me felt like the first lock in a chain I could no longer control. The engine rumbled to life, and just like that, I was driven away — another piece of my life splintering in the rearview mirror.

CHAPTER 20

(J)udgment

I was going back to jail—a place I associated with profound shame, loss of control, and the lowest points of my past—and all the fear and suffocating uncertainty that came with it flooded over me. But this time was different. This wasn't me turning myself in or walking into a courtroom months after an incident. This time, I had been cuffed and escorted out, my life abruptly yanked from my hands in full view of my children and neighbors.

A new wave of dread washed over me in the back of the police car, the plastic seat cold beneath me, as I realized we weren't heading towards the nearby city jail, but were instead merging onto the freeway, heading south towards the much larger, more intimidating county jail. My heart pounded against my ribs like a trapped bird. This wasn't just a minor incident, a temporary setback, a night in the local holding cell. This felt serious.

The bitter, choking irony of the situation gnawed at me relentlessly. My second time heading to jail, while my grandfather— the man who had molested me—had never even glimpsed the inside of a cell. The associates who I believed had intentionally set my car ablaze after I cooperated with police faced no consequences. Andrew, the man who had raped me just a week before, continued to walk free, facing no charges. Nearly every person who had inflicted deep harm on me—through molestation, rape, kidnapping, assault, vandalism, or relentless bullying—had escaped accountability altogether. The only one who had ever faced any consequence was my grandfather, and even then, it was nothing more than a slap on the wrist.

Meanwhile, I felt I had been punished severely, disproportionately, for every single misstep I had ever taken. I wasn't seeking absolution for my actions at Eric's house; I understood losing control had consequences. But the blatant, staggering injustice of the larger picture screamed at me in the confines of the police car. *Where was the fairness in a world that allowed the guilty, the predators, the truly harmful, to roam free while victims, often acting out from trauma, were punished?* It felt like the universe was playing a cruel, cosmic joke, where the scales of justice were irrevocably tipped in favor of the wicked. The weight of this realization pressed down on me, threatening to crush my already fractured spirit. I couldn't help but cry out internally, a silent scream for some semblance of balance, some equality in the distribution of punishment, some sign that my pain mattered.

Being placed in general population at the county jail meant sharing a cramped, cold cell with five other women, a stark, terrifying contrast to the relative solitude of my previous work-release incarceration. Privacy was an unimaginable luxury. The stainless-steel toilet, bolted to the floor with only a low half-wall for modesty, was situated in the open, forcing the most private bodily functions to be performed in full view of cellmates. Eye contact during those moments felt unavoidable, humiliating. Every sound—whispers, coughs, snores, muffled sobs—echoed eerily off the concrete walls and metal bars, leaving one feeling constantly exposed, vulnerable, stripped bare. The experience was a harsh, immediate reminder to abandon any lingering notions of dignity or self-respect. In the cellblock, there was simply no room for such delicate sensibilities; survival meant shutting down, becoming numb.

That night, lying stiffly on the thin, plastic mattress, fear gnawed at me as I began to bleed abnormally, far too soon for my menstrual cycle. Panic tightened my chest. Was it a consequence of the rape a week prior, the internal trauma manifesting physically? Or was it from the harsh impact of being shoved onto the unforgiving concrete earlier that day? Desperate, unsure, and terrified, I called for a guard, my voice trembling as I recounted the horrific assault I had suffered just a week prior and informed him of the alarming, abnormal bleeding. He listened impassively. After what felt like an eternity, an agonizing wait filled with fear and uncertainty, he managed to corroborate my account of the rape report with the detective handling the case. Relief, sharp and immediate, washed over me as they finally transferred me to the relative quiet of the medical unit.

The isolation from the constant noise and observation of the general population was welcome, but the oppressive solitude of the small medical cell soon weighed heavily on my sanity. Left alone with my swirling, terrified thoughts and a Book of Mormon—one of many placed intentionally in every cell, presumably for comfort—I found no solace in its pages. Its teachings only deepened my anguish, amplifying my sense of unworthiness and failure, like salt in an already gaping wound.

The day after my arrest, I was ushered into a waiting room with other inmates and brought before the court for my initial hearing. This appearance would determine whether I'd be granted bail and what the conditions would be. Having learned a bitter lesson from my previous experience with the fake robbery charges—where I pled guilty based on false promises and ended up in jail—I was prepared to plead not guilty when the time came, regardless of the circumstances.

The courtroom was crowded; a large group of prisoners, apparently part of a dismantled criminal organization busted the night before, were being arraigned before me, their faces grim, their charges severe. Most were denied bail. Listening to their cases only heightened my own anxiety.

As my turn approached, my nervousness intensified, my palms sweating. I stood before the judge, feeling small and exposed, as she reviewed my case file, her expression unreadable. She read the charges aloud: unlawful entry, assault, and another charge I can't recall. My ears roared, my vision momentarily blurring, when she mentioned felony charges. Felonies? How could pushing someone and entering a house where my children were constitute felonies? The word itself felt like a life sentence.

As the judge continued reading the arresting officer's report detailing the incident, a puzzled expression slowly crossed her face. She paused, reread a section, and frowned. It became clear, even to me standing there in terror, that the officer who had filed the charges had made a grave error in coding them. After carefully reviewing the officer's own narrative description of the events, the judge concluded definitively that none of the events described warranted felony charges. With a sigh that perhaps held a hint of exasperation at the officer's error, bail was set at a mere $100. Overcome with a dizzying wave of relief, I knew at least I wouldn't have to spend another night in that dreadful place. Freedom, however temporary, felt within reach.

Upon returning home later that day after posting the small bail amount, I was met with more devastating news. Eric and Cindy had already taken legal action, wasting no time in filing a no-contact order against me. The stark white papers stipulated that I was prohibited from seeing or speaking with my boys, except for one supervised weekend visit within the next few weeks, until our scheduled court date. The air rushed out of my lungs. Just days before, my world had revolved around the trauma of the rape—trying to sleep, speaking with detectives, processing the violation. Now, all of that raw, unprocessed trauma had to take a backseat to what felt like the most significant, most terrifying battle of my life: the fight to retain my rights as a mother, the fight to simply see my children.

One condition of eventually getting the no-contact order lifted and regaining access to my children was that I undergo a court-ordered psychological evaluation. It was the most invasive non-physical thing I have ever endured. I felt stripped bare, humiliated beyond belief, as a young man, barely out of college it seemed, asked me intensely personal questions for hours. He probed into the recent rape, my childhood sexual abuse, my failed marriage, my mental health history, my financial struggles—digging into every painful, vulnerable corner of my life, all under the guise of determining if I was a threat to my own children. The unfairness felt suffocating, a cruel irony given the complete lack of consequences for those who had actually harmed me throughout my life.

Yet, I endured the excruciating, demeaning process because I had no choice if I wanted to see my boys. In the end, the evaluation determined that I was neither a threat nor "crazy." It was a small, almost insulting bit of validation after such a degrading ordeal, a tiny win in a battle that felt overwhelmingly unjust and stacked against me.

Because the charges were initially filed as felonies, my case was escalated from the Justice Court to the District Court, a far more intimidating prospect with potentially harsher consequences. The gravity of facing felony charges, even if based on an error, weighed heavily on me. Thankfully, amidst this turmoil, a lifeline appeared. A close friend had recently established a law firm operating on a sliding-scale fee structure, committed to providing quality legal representation regardless of financial means. Her firm and her expertise became invaluable as I navigated the complexities of the District Court system, offering guidance and support when I felt completely overwhelmed and alone.

The outcome of the initial District Court case was unexpected and brought immense relief. The state prosecutor reviewed the file and agreed with the arraignment judge: the evidence simply didn't support felony charges. They dismissed the case entirely at that level. I was overjoyed, tears of relief streaming down my face. I thought the legal nightmare—this specific chapter of it anyway—was finally over.

Unfortunately, I was wrong.

Eric and Cindy, perhaps believing a night in jail, weeks away from my children under a no-contact order, and the humiliation of a psych evaluation wasn't sufficient punishment for my actions that day, decided to pursue the matter further. Unbeknownst to me at the time, my sister had informed Eric about the rape when he called her after my arrest, providing context he and Cindy apparently chose to ignore or disbelieve. They requested that misdemeanor charges be filed against me in the city court based on the exact same incident the District Court had just dismissed. The nightmare rebooted, shifting venues but continuing its relentless assault. A new legal battle, back in the local system, was about to begin.

When I arrived at the city courthouse for this new case, feeling weary but resolute, I was prepared to present my side of the story. I was convinced that if the judge or prosecutor understood the context—the recent rape that had left me traumatized and sleep-deprived, the ongoing custody frustrations, the provocation by Cindy—they would surely show empathy, perhaps even dismiss these lesser charges. However, the proceedings took another unexpected, deflating turn. Before I could even speak, the prosecutor requested a meeting with my lawyer.

During this brief hallway meeting, a plea deal was presented. The terms involved reducing the multiple potential misdemeanor charges to a single count of Disorderly Conduct. It sounded reasonable at first, until the catch: this charge would carry a permanent "domestic violence tag" on my record. In exchange for this "deal," I would have to plead guilty.

The proposition made me feel nauseated, my stomach churning with anxiety. A domestic violence charge? How would I ever secure employment, volunteer at my kids' schools, or even rent an apartment with such a mark against my name? The implications felt daunting, life-altering. My immediate instinct was to decline, to fight, to finally tell my side of the story. I had meticulously reviewed the police reports and witness statements, confident I could expose inconsistencies. Crucially, Eric's statement claimed that I had either "been pushed or fell," a calculated ambiguity that felt like perjury to me. I knew he had pushed me, forcefully. I believed that if I could get him on the witness stand under oath, he would be forced to either tell the truth about the push or commit perjury. Getting that truth on the record felt like the only path to real justice, the only way to counter the narrative being built against me.

My attorney informed me she would follow my instructions but strongly cautioned against rejecting the plea bargain. A trial, she explained, was inherently risky. If a judge or jury didn't believe my context mattered, if they focused solely on the push and me entering the home, and I were found guilty of the original misdemeanor charges, I could face more jail time and substantial fines, potentially impacting my custody situation even further.

Despite my strong convictions, despite feeling it went against everything I believed in, the fear of those harsher consequences, the fear of losing more time with my children, won out. Exhausted by the constant fighting, financially drained, and emotionally depleted, I made the difficult, pragmatic decision to accept the plea deal. I stood before the judge again, my voice barely a whisper, and entered a guilty plea to Disorderly Conduct with a domestic violence tag, acknowledging culpability for my actions that day to avoid the potential for a much harsher sentence.

The fight was over, but the resolution felt hollow, bitter—another injustice layered upon the rest, another instance where my voice felt silenced by the system.

CHAPTER 21

(P)ieces

Now that the criminal case stemming from that awful day at Eric's house was finally resolved, the plea deal accepted and the immediate legal threat behind me, I was able to focus all my energy on the battle that truly mattered: securing equal custody of my boys. The no-contact order had been temporary, lifted after the initial court proceedings and psych evaluation, but establishing a fair and stable long-term custody arrangement felt like staring up at a mountain I wasn't sure I had the strength to climb. I knew it wouldn't be easy, given the animosity and the events that had transpired, and I braced myself for a long and emotionally draining process.

The next few years were fraught with tension, a constant, low-grade warfare conducted primarily through terse emails and text messages. Communication with Eric, especially with Cindy now firmly in the picture, remained incredibly difficult. Simple logistical questions could explode into accusations. There were countless heated exchanges, virtual shouting matches typed out late at night, often filled with immature barbs, unnecessary comments about my parenting or lifestyle, and passive-aggressive digs from both sides.

The stress felt relentless, a constant knot in my stomach. The heartache of reading hurtful words from my ex-husband, the father of my children, brought me to tears more times than I can remember, often leaving me feeling exhausted and defeated before the day even began. The constant conflict, the feeling of having to perpetually fight for my rightful time with my own children, the gnawing financial strain—it felt like trying to swim upstream against a relentless current.

But I refused to give up. My boys were everything to me—my anchor, my reason. I was determined to have a consistent, meaningful, equal presence in their lives. Eventually, after what felt like an eternity of back-and-forth emails between lawyers, tense mediation sessions where civility barely held, and presenting my case for stability and involvement, my persistence paid off. A formal, legal 50/50 custody arrangement was finally granted. Holding that court order felt like a monumental victory—a validation, a crucial step towards rebuilding my life and reclaiming my role as their mother on equal footing.

However, navigating the emotional landscape of my own life remained chaotic. The stability I fought for regarding my children didn't translate internally. To keep my mind occupied during the weeks I didn't have the boys, to avoid confronting the profound discomfort I felt with solitude, the silence of an empty apartment, and the underlying trauma that still simmered beneath the surface, I persisted relentlessly in the dating scene.

It was a coping mechanism—a way to feel wanted, desired, distracted—but it often led directly back to disappointment and reinforced my deepest negative self-perceptions. I'd encounter someone online whose profile seemed captivating, whose initial messages were charming, only to meet in person and discover they fell drastically short of expectations—perhaps they looked nothing like their pictures, or their personality was grating, or worse, they revealed predatory intentions early on.

Alternatively, even if I met someone genuinely remarkable—kind, stable, interesting—my own unresolved issues, my fear of deep emotional intimacy, or my anxious attachment style would inevitably sabotage the connection. I'd either push them away with neediness or pull back abruptly out of fear, ensuring they swiftly lost interest upon realizing the limitations of what I felt I could offer—or perhaps sensing the unresolved chaos swirling within me.

My experiences with online dating during this period were so outlandish, so filled with bizarre characters and near-misses, they could fill an entire book themselves. There was the squatter—a man I dated briefly who, after staying over a few times, simply refused to leave my small apartment for over a week, ignoring my requests, making himself comfortable on my couch until I finally had to threaten police intervention to get him out, leaving me feeling violated and unsafe in my own home.

Then there were the fleeting, almost surreal connections with professional athletes—a Harlem Globetrotter whose travel schedule made anything real impossible, and an MLS player whose messages were exciting but ultimately superficial. Neither resulted in an actual in-person meeting, but they provided me with tickets to their games, allowing me to give my sons some unique, fun experiences amidst the turmoil of our lives—a small silver lining.

I encountered men from literally all walks of life: some were admittedly homeless, living out of their cars (a situation I felt I couldn't judge harshly, given my own recent brush with homelessness), while others were highly successful entrepreneurs or professionals—yet often proved emotionally unavailable, manipulative, or simply looking for something casual when I craved connection.

In one particularly chilling instance, early in these post-divorce dating endeavors, I exchanged several messages over a few weeks with a man who seemed pleasant enough online, if a little intense. We never met in person, the conversation eventually fizzling out. Years later, I saw his face staring out from the local news—he had tragically murdered his girlfriend and then taken his own life. The realization that I had interacted with him, even briefly and superficially online, sent a cold wave of fear through me, highlighting the very real, hidden dangers lurking behind anonymous online profiles and the vulnerability inherent in seeking connection in that space.

These experiences—ranging from the frustratingly mundane to the bizarre to the terrifying—constantly reinforced my deep-seated feelings of inadequacy. *Why did I keep attracting these situations? What was wrong with me?* Yet, paradoxically, no amount of adversity, disappointment, or even genuine danger seemed capable of deterring me from continuing the cycle.

I was desperately seeking connection, validation, love—but looking for it in all the wrong places, through a lens distorted by past hurts and present instability. I was undeniably in the throes of a deep crisis, driven by forces I didn't understand, but it would take years—more therapy, more self-reflection, and more hard lessons—before I could fully grasp the extent of my turmoil and begin the genuine work of healing.

CHAPTER 22

(C)onnection

In September 2015, after years navigating the tumultuous and often disheartening dating scene following my divorce from Eric, I was feeling incredibly jaded. The cycle of hope followed by disappointment, the encounters with men who were unavailable, unkind, or simply incompatible, had taken its toll. I was starting to think that perhaps finding a healthy, lasting relationship just wasn't in the cards for me, that maybe I was destined to be alone. But despite my reservations, the lure of potential connection, however fleeting, drew me back to the familiar, almost mindless swiping left and right on Tinder.

It felt like a monotonous routine, scrolling through mostly uninteresting profiles – blurry photos, cliché bios, faces that blurred into one another – my thumb moving almost automatically out of habit more than hope.

However, amidst the sea of unremarkable faces, one profile caught my eye, making me pause my rapid swiping. The pictures were captivating – not professionally polished, but genuine. He was tall, dark, and handsome, with eyes that held a captivating mix of depth and danger—like he was equal parts good man and bad boy. His smile was effortless, slightly crooked in a way that suggested confidence without arrogance, and his whole presence seemed to hum with an easy charm. Even through the small phone screen, he radiated a kind of grounded magnetism—like someone who'd seen things but hadn't let them harden him. I couldn't help but smile back at the screen as I swiped through them.

But then I came across the last picture, and my enthusiasm wavered significantly. He was wearing an absolutely dreadful hat, the kind that screamed questionable taste, maybe trying too hard to be cool. For a moment, I almost swiped left, letting that superficial judgment override the initial spark of connection. *That hat, though...* Yet, the other pictures were so compelling, something about his energy felt different, lighter, more authentic than most. I decided to take a chance, flicking my thumb right. To my delight, a notification popped up almost immediately: *It's a Match!* A small thrill went through me.

Over the next few days, we engaged in casual conversations via the app's messenger. The banter was easy, comfortable. We got to know each other, sharing snippets of our lives, our interests (discovering a shared love for certain types of music and outdoor activities), and discussing, cautiously, what we were looking for (or perhaps trying to avoid) in a relationship. He asked me out for the upcoming weekend, but I had to decline. It was my designated weekend with my boys, and after the emotional absence described in earlier chapters, I had made a conscious effort to prioritize our time together, to be fully present, rebuilding that connection.

He was completely understanding, showing no signs of impatience or pressure, simply replying, "Okay, family first. How about the following weekend instead?"

Honestly, based on past experiences, I assumed he would lose interest and move on to someone more readily available. Men often lost patience with the complexities of dating a single mom with three kids. But to my surprise, he didn't disappear. He texted again a couple of days later, expressing his continued eagerness to meet me in person. He inquired if there was any chance we could meet up briefly for coffee, even just for an hour, simply to say hello.

Coincidentally, my boys and I already had plans to visit a local farmers market the next day. On a whim, feeling a little bold, half-expecting him to decline the chaotic prospect of meeting not just me but my three active sons right off the bat, I invited him to join us there. I was pleasantly surprised when he readily, even enthusiastically, accepted.

I couldn't recall the specifics of my own attire that Saturday afternoon, probably something comfortable and practical like jeans and a t-shirt, ready for chasing kids around a market. But I remember him arriving, spotting us near the entrance, looking slightly nervous but smiling that slightly crooked smile from his pictures. He wore a classic, laid-back ensemble: faded blue jeans, a Bob Marley t-shirt, and a pair of well-worn Converse sneakers. And thankfully, the dreadful hat from his profile picture was nowhere in sight!

The boys were thoroughly engrossed in their play at the small playground near the market entrance, executing daring tricks on the slide and swings, vying for my attention with shouts of "Mom, watch this!" He greeted them first, crouching down to their level, introducing himself simply as Keith, asking them their names and what they were playing with the same warmth and genuine interest he had shown me in our messages. His undeniable appeal came from his tall stature, striking features (even better in person), and that palpable good man/bad boy vibe. He didn't seem phased by the kid chaos at all.

We decided to stroll through the bustling market together, the boys occasionally running ahead to point at colorful produce or lagging behind to look at handmade crafts. The air was filled with the sounds of chatter, laughter, live folk music from a corner booth, and the smells of fresh bread, kettle corn, and ripe peaches. Within mere minutes of walking side-by-side, weaving through the crowds, surrounded by the vibrant energy, I found myself instinctively wanting to reach for his hand. The impulse was so strong, so surprisingly natural, that I had to consciously pull back, reminding myself to take it slow, to not rush things, to savor the newness and uncertainty.

But there was an undeniable sense of security and comfort in his presence, a feeling of ease I hadn't experienced with a potential romantic partner in a very long time, maybe ever.

We spent an enchanting hour or so exploring the market stalls, sampling local honey that dripped from tiny wooden spoons, admiring handmade pottery, laughing as the boys tried to guess the weight of a giant pumpkin. As the sun began to dip lower, casting a warm, golden glow over the thinning crowds and signaling the market's closing time, he tentatively asked, "Would you guys maybe want to grab some dinner?"

His invitation, including the boys without hesitation, was met with an enthusiastic yes from me (and definite cheers from the kids). We embarked on a delightful culinary adventure at a nearby family-friendly pizza place.

Following a truly enjoyable meal filled with easy laughter, shared stories, and surprisingly little awkwardness, he insisted on accompanying us back to our car, ensuring our safe return as dusk settled. His chivalrous gestures – holding doors, making sure the boys didn't run into the parking lot, walking on the outside of the sidewalk – felt genuine, ingrained, not performative.

As we reached my badly battered car, he enveloped me in a warm, lingering embrace, his genuine care evident in the crinkles around his kind, dark brown eyes. "When can I see you next?" he inquired, his voice filled with an anticipation that mirrored my own.

A flutter of butterflies erupted in my stomach, the good kind this time, hopeful and light.

CHAPTER 23

(W)ashington

The very next day, demonstrating an eagerness that was both flattering and slightly terrifying given my history of rushing things, he graciously joined us for Sunday dinner at my parents' house. The atmosphere was thick with my parents' understandable caution, given my past romantic misadventures. My dad, ever the grill master, immediately put Keith to work, handing him tongs and assigning him burger-flipping duties – perhaps a subtle test. Keith proved himself more than capable, handling the task and my dad's scrutiny with easy confidence and humor. Over perfectly grilled burgers and potato salad, my parents seemed to relax, taking a genuine liking to him, drawn in by his easygoing nature and respectful demeanor. My boys were also clearly quite fond of him already, laughing at his jokes, showing him their toys, and including him naturally in their chatter. And as for me, watching him interact so effortlessly with my family, seeing him fit so comfortably into my world, well, I was completely smitten.

Later that night, after the boys were tucked into bed, under the twinkling stars of a cool fall evening, standing on the familiar front porch where I had often sought solace and clarity during difficult times, the scent of autumn leaves in the air, we shared our first kiss. It wasn't rushed or demanding; it was gentle, tentative at first, then deepening with a warmth that spread through my entire body. As our lips met, it wasn't just passion I felt, but a profound sense of warmth, safety, and belonging washing over me. It felt different from any kiss before. In his arms, I felt a sense of home, a feeling I had desperately longed for but never truly found in a romantic partner. He felt like home.

Keith and I quickly became inseparable after that weekend. It felt like we spent nearly every waking moment together over the next few weeks and months, texting constantly when apart, finding excuses to see each other, integrating him seamlessly into my life with the boys. Our connection felt so strong, so right, so different from anything before, that we began discussing marriage, perhaps foolishly fast, within a mere month of dating. He would playfully call me Mrs. Washington, and I couldn't help but blush, cherishing the sound of it, the implication of a shared, stable future. It felt like we were destined to be together, two souls finally finding their match after long, difficult journeys.

At the time, he was living in a small one-bedroom apartment in Salt Lake City, while I was residing temporarily in Orem with my parents. His apartment wasn't spacious enough to accommodate my three growing boys on overnights, and the drive between Salt Lake and Utah County, especially with my demanding early morning shifts at the local grocery store (often requiring me to wake up as early as

3:00 a.m.), was becoming a practical challenge to maintaining the constant connection we both craved.

To bridge the distance and make our burgeoning relationship more manageable, Keith made the significant step of moving in temporarily with my brother, who also lived in Orem, that December. This arrangement, while not ideal, brought us physically closer and allowed us to spend more consistent time together as a potential family unit, testing the waters of blending our lives.

After a few months of him living with my brother, saving money and solidifying our commitment, Keith and I were finally able to afford our own place together – a modest apartment, but it was ours. Finding and moving into that home was a momentous occasion. It marked the first time since my divorce years earlier that my boys had their own bedrooms again, with actual beds they could call their own, not just mattresses on the floor or shared spaces. The stability and comfort of establishing our own home together, picking out curtains, arranging furniture, creating a shared space, brought an immense sense of joy and relief to all of us. It felt like we were finally building something solid, something lasting.

The morning of our wedding day in March 2017 arrived, and ironically, after years of dreaming of this moment, I woke up feeling absolutely terrible. I'm usually not one to get sick to my stomach, but Murphy's Law dictated that on the day I was supposed to marry the man I believed was the man of my dreams, I found myself hunched over the toilet, praying to the porcelain god, begging for relief. Nausea had woken me extra early, disrupting my plans for a calm, relaxed morning. In between bouts of sickness, feeling shaky and miserable, I wrapped myself in a blanket and sat on our small balcony, watching the sun begin to rise over the Wasatch mountains, painting the pre-dawn sky with breathtaking hues of amber, purple, and pink. Pen in hand, a legal pad balanced on my knees, I decided to write my wedding vows.

As I wrote, the words flowing surprisingly easily despite my physical discomfort, I reflected on the winding, often painful paths that had led us both to this improbable moment. Keith had never been married before. His own childhood had been marked by instability; his father left when he was young, and his mother joined the Air Force to provide a better life, taking them far away from their roots in Detroit. Their journey had taken them across the United States and even overseas, where they were stationed in Japan for a few years. Keith eventually followed in his mother's footsteps, joining the Air Force himself, serving for four years before a knee injury led to an early medical discharge.

We both carried scars, different but deep. We both understood the cracks in each other's pasts, the weight of difficult experiences, the longing for stability. Our journeys were different, but we had both been broken by life's trials in our own ways. We both longed for a safe haven, a partnership where we could find trust, love, unwavering support, and true friendship. And miraculously, it felt like we had found that in each other. Our fractured souls seemed to recognize each other, drawing us together, creating a safe space where we could finally begin to heal, together.

As I sat on the balcony that chilly morning, the rising sun warming my face, the words of my vows flowed from me as easily and naturally as the tears of gratitude and overwhelming hope that accompanied them.

On a September day in 2012, at thirty-one years old, I was sitting in my room listening to music, feeling utterly lost and hopeless. It had been exactly a year, another September, since I had made the life-changing decision to leave my first marriage. One I knew was right, but sitting there that day, one year later, facing the daunting reality of single motherhood and financial struggle, I felt hopeless. Taylor Swift's "Innocent" began to play on the radio, and as I listened, tears streaming down my face, I suddenly felt she had written the song just for me.

It's okay, life is a tough crowd. Thirty-two and still growing up now. Who you are is not what you did, you're still an innocent.

Time turns flames to embers, you'll have new Septembers, every one of us has messed up too.

Minds change like the weather, I hope you remember, today is never too late to be brand new.

I remember thinking in that moment, clinging to that fragile hope, My Mr. Right is out there somewhere, waiting for his Mrs. Right, and I'm just not her yet. But maybe, someday, I could be.

It would take a few more Septembers, filled with more mistakes, more heartbreak, more healing, but on September 26, 2015, Mr. Right showed up for a date at the farmers market with me... and three energetic boys in tow. I'll never forget the excitement that swept through me, the nervous energy, the good-feeling butterflies fluttering in my tummy. Within the first ten minutes, I caught myself wanting to reach for your hand and having to tell myself to chill, to not screw this up. It just felt so natural, so easy.

The very next day, you held my hand, and later that night, we shared our first kiss on my parents' porch. I felt alive with feelings I had never experienced before—not just feelings of love and intense excitement, but of profound security and deep peace as well.

I have spent every day since falling more and more in love with you. I am often in awe of you, Keith, and the way you show love so selflessly, so patiently. You have been there for the good and the bad, in sickness (literally, today!) and in health. Just three weeks ago, we sat side by side in a sterile hospital room as our son Scott received his Type 1 Diabetes diagnosis, learning all we could to prepare us both to care for him, and all I could think amidst the fear and worry was, Man! This guy drew the short straw. Run! But I knew, deep down, you weren't going anywhere. You love us. All of us. And us loves you.

You have shown this girl, who was once so sure she was destined to never know anything more than a mediocre, painful love, that the fairy tale, weak-in-the-knees kind of love certainly does exist. And more importantly, that I am deserving of such love. In you, Mr. Washington, I have found my W.

Our wedding day, the one I had dreamt about for years, turned out to be far from the picture-perfect fairytale I had envisioned in some ways. The morning started with that relentless wave of nausea that never fully subsided. My hair and makeup, which I had hoped would make me feel like a radiant princess, looked nothing short of disastrous in my stressed-out, overly critical eyes. By the end of the night, after the ceremony, the reception, the mingling, I was utterly exhausted, still feeling sick, and emotionally overwhelmed. But amidst the minor chaos and the superficial disappointments, there was one moment, one feeling, that shone through, that truly mattered. It was the moment I stood facing my husband, hearing his voice, thick with emotion, filled with love and devotion, as he spoke his vows to me.

"I didn't know how enjoyable a walk in the park would be until the day I met you. I also didn't know how much I would fall in love with you since then. I cherish every moment, every kiss, every smile, every frown. Just to be able to have the chance to make you smile, to kiss you, to love you, brings me joy. I promise to love you the way the Lord intended His men to love their wives. Here and in Heaven. I pray He brings us many more walks, talks, smiles, and frowns. As long as we do it together. I love you so much Mrs. Washington. So much."

We do. Forever and ever. Or so I believed with all my heart on that imperfectly perfect day.

CHAPTER 24

(P)ersistence

When Keith and I first crossed paths, neither of us was exactly rolling in dough. I was barely scraping by, earning a meager $9 an hour as a cashier at a local grocery store. The constant beeping of the scanner, the smell of ripe bananas mingling with cleaning supplies, the endless stream of faces – it wasn't glamorous, but it kept the lights on. I told myself it was temporary, just a stepping stone until I found something better. But somewhere between bagging groceries and counting change, I began to notice something unexpected: possibility. Watching supervisors manage inventory, handle customer complaints, and oversee staff, I started to think that maybe, with hard work, I could do that too.

Driven by this newfound ambition and the growing stability of my relationship with Keith, I transitioned to full-time employment at the grocery store. I seized every opportunity to cross-train and expand my skill set, eager to prove my worth and climb the ladder. I learned the complexities of the customer service desk, handling returns and complaints with a smile. I became the backup bookkeeper, meticulously counting cash and balancing drawers in the small, windowless back office. Being entrusted with handling large sums of cash, often alone in that quiet office, felt significant. It was a quiet act of healing for the part of me that carried the shame of orchestrating the fast-food robbery as a troubled teen. Despite the opportunity, I was never even tempted to steal; the responsibility felt like a chance to prove, mostly to myself, that I was no longer that person. I took on any shift available—overnight cashier shifts in the echoing quiet, early mornings at the bookkeeping desk starting as early as 4 a.m., holidays when most people were home with their families, and busy weekend rushes—anything to gain valuable hours, prove my commitment, and build experience.

For the most part, I genuinely enjoyed aspects of the work, especially the brief, friendly interactions with regular customers. There were still awkward moments, of course – encountering someone I didn't like from my past, or someone I knew harbored ill feelings towards me, their judgmental gaze lingering a moment too long as I bagged their groceries. These interactions were uncomfortable reminders of the life and reputation I was trying to move beyond, but they felt like a small price to pay for the overall positive experience and the sense of purpose the job provided. In a surprising and heartwarming turn of events, I even reconnected with my old manager from the fast food place I had helped rob when I was 18. She was working full-time at the grocery store now. Years had passed since I confessed, and she had shown me incredible kindness and understanding during that difficult time. Seeing her familiar face, working alongside her again, felt like a small, healing circle closing, a quiet acknowledgment of how far I'd come.

After months of dedicated hard work, consistently exceeding expectations, feeling confident in my abilities within that context, I decided to apply for a promotion to supervisor. I carefully filled out the application, highlighting my cross-training and willingness to work any shift. Unfortunately, my application was unsuccessful; the position went to someone else with more seniority. The rejection left me feeling deeply discouraged and defeated, amplifying old feelings of inadequacy. *See? Not good enough.* The disappointment was compounded by the stark realization that I simply could not continue to support my family adequately on my current meager salary. The dream of managing the grocery store suddenly felt insufficient, a dead end.

Just as I was grappling with this setback, feeling stuck and unsure of my next move, opportunity knocked, albeit softly, through the unexpected avenue of social media. One evening, mindlessly scrolling through Facebook, I stumbled upon a post from a former schoolmate I hadn't seen in years. He mentioned that his company, a local tech company specializing in software, was hiring for customer service representative positions and encouraged anyone interested to contact him. Intrigued by this seemingly serendipitous opening, a potential escape from retail, I reached out, sending a hesitant message.

He explained that the role wasn't a typical call center job but rather a position supporting enterprise software clients – a world completely foreign to me, filled with jargon I didn't understand. He couldn't provide specific details about the salary but assured me that he enjoyed his work, the company culture was good, and he would be happy to refer me. Despite the lack of concrete information and my own significant self-doubt about qualifying for a "tech" job with only retail and some call center experience from years ago, the prospect of something new, something potentially better-paying, something different, filled me with a renewed sense of fragile hope.

The morning of the interview, however, I woke up consumed by dread and defeat. The familiar weight of anticipated rejection settled heavily upon me. It felt like I had been stuck in an endless loop of job applications and interviews for years. The cumulative weight of these disappointments had left me questioning my worth, wondering if even attending this interview was a futile endeavor. The thought of putting on uncomfortable clothes, driving to Provo, forcing a smile, answering questions, only to face another disheartening silence, felt almost too much to bear. I seriously considered giving up, canceling, and staying in bed.

Then, a small but persistent voice inside my head, the one that sometimes pushed me forward despite the fear, spoke up, cutting through the negativity. It said, *Amber, you have no right to complain about the opportunities you're not getting if you're not even willing to try.* That seemingly insignificant internal nudge became the catalyst for a profound shift. I pushed past the fear, put on my best interview outfit, and went.

The office environment felt sterile and serious—plain, but with an unmistakable air of importance. It was a stark contrast to the grocery store breakroom, with its scuffed linoleum floors and constant chatter. Here, the atmosphere was quieter, more focused. People sat upright at their desks, typing intently, the hum of productivity filling the space. It didn't feel like just a job—it felt like a career. The interview itself couldn't have gone better. I connected with the hiring manager, David, finding him surprisingly tall and down-to-earth. I answered the questions honestly, drawing parallels between customer service in retail and supporting software clients, emphasizing my work ethic and willingness to learn. For perhaps the first time in a professional setting, I felt a sense of competence, of articulating my skills effectively. To my utter astonishment, at the end of the conversation, he offered me the position right then and there, with a starting pay rate of $17 an hour – nearly double what I was making. I was completely taken aback; my jaw nearly dropped. I quickly composed myself, trying to appear professional, careful not to show my shock lest he reconsider or lower the offer.

There was a catch, though. The position was only temporary, a three-month contract to cover an employee's maternity leave. Initially, disappointment flickered – just temporary? But then practicality took over. I realized I could, theoretically, keep my job at the grocery store, working nights, and take on this temporary role during the day. It would mean juggling two jobs again, a prospect I didn't relish, remembering the burnout from years before. But it represented a significant pay increase and, crucially, an opportunity to gain valuable experience in a completely new industry, a potential escape route. I accepted.

During my initial training period at the tech company, sitting in brightly lit training rooms learning about software I barely understood, I found myself working alongside two other new hires. One had secured a full-time, permanent position; the other was also full-time but on a temporary contract like mine, with the possibility of permanent employment after a trial period. Both were notably younger than me, fresh out of college, seemingly navigating this corporate world with an ease I didn't possess. It quickly became apparent that my approach differed significantly from theirs. While they often seemed distracted, sneaking texts on their phones under the table or scrolling social media during presentations, I was fully absorbed, diligently taking notes in a fresh notebook, asking clarifying questions, determined to make the most of this chance, terrified of failing.

Observing their casual attitude, their seeming lack of urgency, I started to contemplate my own prospects. Could I, with enough dedication and hard work, prove myself indispensable? Could I potentially secure a permanent position, perhaps even the one held by the other temporary employee? Driven by this ambition, fueled by the fear of returning to minimum-wage uncertainty, and perhaps by a competitive spirit I didn't know I had, I set out on a mission.

I volunteered for the less desirable graveyard shift when the opportunity arose, seeing it not just as a burden, but as a chance to demonstrate commitment and interact with different teams and managers. I adopted a proactive approach, constantly asking questions, seeking information beyond the basic training materials, trying to understand the *why* behind the processes. I made a conscious effort to contribute thoughtfully in meetings, sharing observations from my unique perspective as someone new to the industry but experienced in customer interaction. I focused on truly understanding customer needs, listening patiently to their frustrations, ensuring their issues were resolved or escalated appropriately, often staying late to follow up. I was determined to excel, confident for perhaps the first time in my professional life that my work ethic and people skills could translate into success in this new environment.

My dedication paid off. I was eventually offered the other temporary position when it became available, the one with the stated possibility of becoming permanent. By this point, feeling more secure in my abilities and exhausted from the two-job juggle, I had left my job at the grocery store. Taking the temp-to-hire role was still a significant risk; it didn't include benefits. My sons were covered under Eric's insurance, but I would be without health coverage myself. Despite the risk, I accepted, optimistic that this was the right path, betting on myself.

It wasn't the kind of leap that made headlines, but for me, it was monumental—a quiet act of defiance against every voice that said I'd never make it beyond the life I'd known. I didn't realize it yet, but this single yes would set me on a path that would change everything.

CHAPTER 25

(A)mbition

What began as a three-month temp job had stretched into almost two years. I had proven myself over and over, but the promise of a permanent position kept getting pushed back, always "next quarter." When it finally came through, I felt like I could exhale for the first time in years. A steady paycheck. Benefits. A career I hadn't even known to dream of before. I was building something I could be proud of, and for the first time in a long time, my life felt like it was moving forward. I didn't know it yet, but this chapter wouldn't be defined only by career growth—it would also deliver a moment I'd been chasing for years: a family trip to the ocean.

Not long after I accepted the permanent position, my manager, David, dropped a bombshell: he was leaving our current tech employer to join its recent enterprise software spin-off. This newly independent company, SUSE, had previously been a division within our firm but was now operating on its own, focusing on a specific software suite. He had been instrumental in securing my permanent role, persistently advocating for me for over a year until he succeeded. His departure felt like losing a key supporter, a mentor, and I worried about my future stability within the company without his backing.

A few weeks after his announcement, however, my phone rang. It was him. His call would, once again, dramatically alter the course of my career. He told me the Maintenance Renewals team had openings – a sales position. He explained the role: I'd be responsible for creating sales quotes, negotiating renewals, and working with existing enterprise customers to ensure they continued their software subscriptions. My initial reaction was disbelief, almost laughter. Sales? Me? With my background? The suggestion felt absurd. I couldn't fathom why anyone would hire me for a sales role; I pictured aggressive, slick-talking salespeople, a world away from my customer service background. But then he mentioned the potential salary – nearly double my current earnings. My jaw dropped for the second time in my interactions with him. That little voice of encouragement, the one that had pushed me to the first tech interview, resurfaced, stronger this time, tinged with excitement: *What have you got to lose? Go for it!* And so, pushing past the familiar tendrils of self-doubt and imposter syndrome, I took the leap and applied for the sales position, and got it.

Life outside of work was also beginning to feel more stable, more joyful during this period. For years, I had been promising my boys an unforgettable beach vacation, a real one, not just a day trip to a local reservoir. Year after year, financial constraints or personal chaos forced me to postpone, always promising "next year." Finally, in

2018, with my career stabilizing and life feeling a bit more manageable, "next year" arrived.

After much searching online, comparing rentals, I found a perfect beach house right on the water's edge in California, close enough for family to join. My parents decided to stay with us in the beach house, while my sisters, brother, and their families opted for a nearby hotel, making it a true extended family vacation. We spent most of our time enjoying the simple pleasures of the beach – the feeling of warm sand between our toes, the rhythmic crash of waves, the salty spray on our skin. We built elaborate sandcastles with moats, splashed and shrieked in the cool Pacific waves, collected pockets full of smooth sea glass and interesting shells. We dedicated one day to the manufactured magic and overwhelming crowds of Universal Studios, a treat for the boys, with the enchanting world of Harry Potter being a favorite.

On our first evening at the beach house, I stepped out onto the wooden porch just as the sun was beginning to set. The horizon glowed in hues of gold and lavender, casting long shadows across the sand. Below, silhouetted against the shimmering ocean, sat Keith, my dad, my brother, and my three boys. They were settled into the provided beach chairs, looking out at the waves, chatting amongst themselves.

The salty breeze lifted my hair as I leaned against the railing, watching them. The sound of their voices, the rhythm of the waves, the sight of all the men I loved most in one place—it filled me with something I hadn't felt in a long time: peace.

Tears welled up unexpectedly, not from sadness or grief, but from a deep, swelling gratitude. Gratitude for moments like this. For healing I never thought I'd experience. For the family that stayed. For a love that lasted.

And for the first time in years, I believed that wholeness might actually last. But life has a way of testing the foundations you build—sometimes sooner than you're ready for.

CHAPTER 26

(R)esilience

The sun was gone, but the image of that evening on the porch—waves rolling in, my boys' laughter blending with my dad's voice—was burned into my memory. It was peace, pure and simple. I had no idea it would be calm before the storm.

The journey to this point, to that simple moment of peace, family, and togetherness, had been so long, so incredibly arduous, filled with countless roadblocks, wrong turns, financial struggles, and moments where I doubted I'd ever find my way to feeling content. The countless instances where I'd had to swallow my pride, eat humble pie, pick myself up from rock bottom, and keep going only served to make that moment, that feeling of simple, uncomplicated happiness, that much sweeter. It had felt like, finally, things were truly falling into place, like I could finally breathe.

My career continued to evolve. My initial year as a customer service representative had been a steep learning curve; it took a full twelve months before I felt truly comfortable and confident navigating the systems and customer issues. Transitioning to the renewal rep role presented another significant challenge – new processes, new pressures, the need to negotiate and close deals. It wasn't until my second year in that role that I felt fully proficient, truly owning my portfolio.

During my first partial year in sales (starting halfway through the fiscal year), I exceeded my quota significantly, achieving over 100%. However, I knew I had inherited many deals initiated by the previous rep, which simply closed under my name during that initial period. While pleased with the result, I didn't feel it accurately reflected my own capabilities yet. In the subsequent full fiscal year, my first full year managing my own quota from start to finish, I fell slightly short. It was frustrating, especially after feeling like I was finally hitting my stride, but I later discovered my quota hadn't been calculated correctly due to internal system errors. Had it been accurate, my sales figures would have comfortably surpassed the target – a small vindication.

As the fiscal year 2020 began, I felt genuinely confident in my ability to succeed in sales. The quota issues seemed resolved, I understood my customers and the renewal process intimately, and I felt ready to have my best year yet. But then, the world changed.

The COVID-19 pandemic hit, bringing unprecedented uncertainty, fear, and disruption to businesses globally. For months, whispers and rumors of layoffs circulated constantly within the company, despite management reassurances that jobs were secure. We tried to focus on hitting our numbers, supporting our customers through their own pandemic challenges, but the anxiety lingered, a heavy cloud of uncertainty hanging over every virtual team meeting.

The fiscal year ended, as usual, on Halloween. We submitted our final numbers, hoping for the best. Just two days later I received the dreaded meeting invitation from my manager, the subject line vague. My stomach plummeted. The call confirmed our worst fears. The company was downsizing due to the pandemic's severe economic impact. Those of us with smaller dollar portfolios, deemed less critical perhaps, including me, were being laid off, effective immediately.

The news felt like the wind had been knocked out of me, leaving me gasping for air. Keith and I had just purchased our first home together only months before, a beautiful house that symbolized the stability and security we thought we'd finally achieved. Now, it felt like we were going to lose everything we had worked so hard for. Keith had a stable job with the school district, but our mortgage and living expenses absolutely required two incomes. Panic, cold and sharp, set in.

In that state of panic, my mind racing, my first instinct was to reach out to my former manager and mentor, David. I texted him, my thumbs trembling, explaining the situation, asking desperately if he knew of any open positions, anywhere within his company. He responded almost immediately, his message a beacon of hope in the sudden darkness. Yes, there was an opening on his team at SUSE. He thought I would be perfect for it.

The subsequent fortnight was another intense emotional whirlwind, swinging dramatically between the despair of the layoff – the fear, the uncertainty, the blow to my confidence – and the elation of new possibilities. I found myself grappling with the unexpected, almost unbelievable dilemma of choosing between two exceptional job offers that materialized quickly.

SUSE offered me the position on David's team – a significant salary increase from my previous role, and the continued benefit of being fully remote. Simultaneously, another tech company, impressed by my resume, extended an offer; their salary wasn't quite as high, and it was a hybrid role requiring some in-office time, but they were enticing new hires with an all-expenses-paid trip to Hawaii in just a few weeks for a company meeting. If I joined before their departure, I'd be included.

Although the Hawaii-bound company had extended their offer first, I paused. The lure of a free trip to Hawaii was incredibly tempting, an escape I desperately craved after the stress of the layoff. But this time, remembering past lessons, I was determined to prioritize my own long-term needs and career goals, rather than being swayed by short-term perks or concerns about disappointing the recruiters at the other company.

The decision wasn't easy. SUSE offered higher pay, the stability of working with a colleague I trusted, and the flexibility of being fully remote, which was invaluable as a mother. The other company offered adventure and a potentially exciting new environment. Weighing my options, reflecting on what truly mattered for my family and my career trajectory, I knew financial security and the freedom of remote work aligned better with my life and aspirations.

I accepted the offer from SUSE, feeling a profound sense of resilience, gratitude, and perhaps a touch of bewildered amusement at the strange twists and turns of fate.

SUSE provided me with opportunities that surpassed my wildest dreams. I used to sit in airports during my rare personal travels, people-watching, fascinated by the confident business travelers navigating terminals with their sleek, coordinated carry-on suitcases and laptop bags. They always seemed impeccably dressed in suits or skirts, taking important calls on their cell phones, receiving updates as they disembarked from flights. I would often wonder about the nature of their work, what important deals they were closing, and how they were fortunate enough to have their travel expenses covered by their employers. I aspired to that life, that level of professional success and freedom.

And suddenly, somehow, almost unbelievably, I had become one of them.

In November 2021, this new reality culminated in an unforgettable journey: my company organized its annual sales summit in the enchanting, almost mythical principality of Monaco. It was my first international trip ever, made even more surreal by the lingering complexities of the global pandemic. Despite the travel hurdles and anxieties, I was determined not to miss this incredible opportunity.

Monaco had always seemed like a fairytale destination, a place of glamour and beauty I'd only seen in movies. Adding immeasurably to the joy, I had recently helped two of my sisters secure jobs with the company, and they were able to join me on this trip of a lifetime.

The five days we spent there were filled with magical moments that still feel dreamlike. Exploring the charming, winding streets of the old town, taking in the breathtaking landscapes of the Mediterranean coast, indulging in delicious local cuisine (so much fresh seafood!), visiting iconic landmarks like the opulent Prince's Palace and the legendary Monte Carlo Casino (where we even played a few rounds of blackjack), strolling along the picturesque harbor lined with unbelievably luxurious yachts – every moment felt like a feast for the senses, a world away from my everyday life.

There were mishaps, of course – both my sister and I, perhaps overwhelmed by the excitement, managed clumsy tumbles on the cobblestone streets – but nothing could dampen our spirits. Dipping my feet into the surprisingly warm, crystal-clear turquoise waters of the Mediterranean Sea felt like pure bliss, a moment of serene contentment, the sun warm on my skin, the gentle breeze in my hair. Reflecting on it, I still feel a sense of awe.

It felt like a dream come true, a tangible symbol of how far I had come – from the depths of despair and instability to this place of professional success and personal joy.

I had reached a place I once thought was unreachable. But the truth is, the higher you climb, the more there is to lose—and my next chapter would prove that no success is ever completely safe.

CHAPTER 27

(M)anifestations

T he successes in my career and the joy of experiences like the Monaco trip were bright spots, moments where life felt full of possibility, proving I could achieve external stability. Yet stability in the outside world didn't erase the battles still raging inside me. One in particular had shadowed my entire life — an enduring, physically demanding, and emotionally loaded struggle with obesity. This was a fight waged not just against weight, but against the deeply ingrained coping patterns, self-worth issues, and trauma responses that had shaped my relationship with food for as long as I could remember.

Just as I had once pushed through fear to take the leap into a tech interview I didn't think I could win, or risked leaving the grocery store for a temp job that could have ended in nothing, I would have to summon that same grit for my health. This battle would require persistence in an entirely different arena — one where the opponent lived inside my own mind and body.

Growing up, my mom was very health-conscious, a stark contrast to the typical pantries of my friends. Our budget for food was limited, making eating out a rare and exciting treat. Our cupboards were devoid of the usual childhood staples: sugary sodas, salty chips, colorful breakfast cereals shaped like cartoon characters, bags of candy. Birthdays were marked by the extraordinary privilege of choosing one box of sugary cereal, a simple pleasure that felt like winning the lottery. I remember agonizing over the choice between Lucky Charms or Captain Crunch.

Despite my mom's diligent efforts to provide healthy meals, or perhaps because of the very restriction, my sisters and I developed an insatiable craving for the forbidden treats. Any opportunity to indulge in processed foods, sugary drinks, or fast food was met with unbridled enthusiasm. Babysitting gigs became synonymous with raiding the family's pantry and fridge, scarfing down cookies or chips in secret before the parents returned. The money I earned was quickly squandered at the corner grocery store on candy bars and sodas. I even recall, with a hot flush of shame, once stealing an old, folded $10 bill from my dad's collection box, oblivious to its potential collector's value, and spending every cent at the local taco joint on greasy bean burritos and cinnamon twists. By high school, with friends who could drive, my babysitting money primarily fueled my burgeoning fast-food addiction – late-night runs for burgers and fries becoming a regular ritual. Food became comfort, rebellion, and readily available pleasure.

I wasn't actually overweight as a child, but I was always taller than the other kids my age, which often made me look—and feel—bigger. I stopped growing in junior high, so by the time I reached high school, I wasn't taller anymore, just thicker. Even then, I wasn't fat.

Not by today's standards. I was the kind of thick that's considered normal—even attractive—now. But back then, in the cruel social hierarchy of adolescence, I might as well have been obese.

The changes brought on by puberty made me more self-conscious, especially as I began to carry weight differently. The reflection in the mirror didn't match the impossibly thin ideals plastered across magazines or celebrated at school. And while today I might have been called curvy or voluptuous, back then it just felt like one more thing that set me apart. One more reason to feel less than. One more mark against me.

During my pregnancy with Scott, I experienced a significant weight gain 75 pounds added to my frame. I was young and naive enough about postpartum bodies to believe the weight would effortlessly melt away after childbirth, like celebrity magazines seemed to promise. Unfortunately, that was not the case. After Scott was born, I was left with a persistent pouch, loose skin, and pounds that clung stubbornly. It was around this time, during a routine check-up, that a doctor first used the clinical term: I was officially categorized, according to BMI charts, as obese. The word landed heavily. Over the next decade, through my marriage to Eric, subsequent pregnancies with William and Owen, and the stresses of daily life, I continued to gain weight steadily, eventually reaching the point of morbid obesity. The physical discomfort – aching joints, difficulty tying my shoes, constant fatigue – became my unwelcome normal.

There were periods of determined effort. Through a combination of intense diet and exercise during my first marriage, fueled by a desire to feel attractive or perhaps regain some sense of control, I managed to lose over 80 pounds. I felt strong, capable, proud of the discipline. However, following my divorce from Eric, plunged back into instability, single parenthood, and emotional turmoil, I experienced a devastating setback. The weight returned with alarming speed, bringing friends – an additional 70 pounds piled onto the weight I had already regained. The cycle felt vicious, inescapable.

When I first met Keith, my weight had reached a staggering 295 pounds. I had managed to delude myself, employing mental gymnastics to avoid the stark reality, believing that as long as the scale didn't actually tip over the 300 mark, I was somehow still within an acceptable, manageable range. This was a dangerous misconception, a denial fueled by shame. I was far from healthy. The strain on my joints made walking painful, stairs felt like mountains, I was constantly short of breath, and fatigue was my constant companion. These were all clear signs that I was pushing my body far beyond its limits. I felt like I was living on borrowed time, and the interest on that physical debt was about to come due in terrifying ways, impacting not just me, but the health scares surrounding my children as well.

In 2017, my oldest son Scott received the life-altering diagnosis of juvenile type 1 diabetes after a frightening episode of diabetic ketoacidosis (DKA) that landed him in the hospital for several days. Our world shifted focus to stabilizing his blood sugar, learning to count carbs, administer insulin shots, prick fingers constantly – immersing ourselves in the relentless demands of managing his chronic condition. Two years later, another health crisis struck as Scott was admitted to the ICU for 5 harrowing days with a severe kidney infection. His condition was critical, septic, his frail body fighting a terrifying battle. The doctors were perplexed by the underlying cause. It took another year, filled with tests and specialists, before we finally received a diagnosis: a rare genetic bladder disorder with no known cure. These experiences – the constant worry, the hospital vigils, the stress related to my son's significant health challenges – undoubtedly added another heavy layer of complexity to my own ongoing health struggles. Stress eating became an easy, albeit destructive, coping mechanism.

After finally securing decent health insurance through my employment with the first tech company, I began seriously exploring the option of weight loss surgery. The idea had crossed my mind numerous times over the years, but it always seemed financially out of reach. There were also times, fueled by societal judgment or my own internalized shame, where I managed to convince myself that opting for surgery was taking the easy way out, that I should possess the willpower to achieve my weight loss goals through sheer determination and discipline alone. The truth, I was slowly realizing, was that losing weight wasn't the primary issue; I had done it before. Maintaining weight loss, fighting against what felt like my body's natural set point and my ingrained emotional eating patterns, was the real, seemingly insurmountable challenge.

Just as I was preparing for a scheduled sleeve gastrectomy surgery in early 2019, having already started the difficult 30-day pre-op liquid diet (a miserable regimen of protein shakes and broth that left me constantly hungry and irritable), a new, terrifying health crisis emerged. A persistent ache began deep in my left calf, intensifying over several hours at work. It wasn't a sharp pain, but a deep, throbbing pulse. Fearing a blood clot, my anxiety spiking, I rushed to the ER. Despite my concerns, the initial exam showed no swelling or redness, and an ultrasound came back clear. The doctor, seemingly dismissive, diagnosed a muscle strain and sent me home with instructions to rest. I felt foolish, embarrassed for having panicked.

Over the following weekend, while on a family getaway, I struggled with increasing shortness of breath, attributing it to the restrictive liquid diet and fatigue. A few days later, back at work during a mandatory training session, the breathing difficulty worsened significantly, accompanied now by sharp, stabbing pains in my chest. Convinced I was being overly dramatic, perhaps even hypochondriacal after the "false alarm" at the ER, I stubbornly sat through the entire day of training, trying to breathe shallowly, hiding my discomfort. Afterwards, finally acknowledging something was seriously wrong, I contacted the nurse overseeing my pre-op care. Hearing my symptoms, her voice sharp with urgency, she instructed me to get to a hospital immediately. Still stubborn, perhaps defiant, I drove myself, deliberately avoiding the ER that had dismissed my concerns earlier. Thirty minutes later, after pulling into the ambulance bay of a different hospital, barely able to walk from the car, I was rushed into an examination room. X-rays and blood work confirmed the gravity of the situation: I had multiple pulmonary emboli, blood clots that had traveled to my lungs, a condition that tragically claims the lives of approximately 100,000 Americans each year.

My doctor concluded the clot likely originated in my leg (despite the clear ultrasound) and was probably a rare but serious side effect of the birth control medication I was taking – not for contraception (I'd had a tubal ligation after Owen's birth), but prescribed to manage heavy, debilitating bleeding that had started after a frightening incident months prior where I thought I was dying. That incident, it turned out, was caused by a uterine polyp. An ablation procedure had been recommended, but the initial diagnostic exam was so excruciatingly painful that fear overwhelmed me. I canceled the ablation, burying my head in the sand, hoping the issue would resolve itself. Unfortunately, ignoring the problem, neglecting my health due to fear, had almost cost me my life.

The pulmonary embolism forced me to postpone the weight loss surgery for several months while I recovered, taking blood thinners and carefully monitoring my health. As the rescheduled surgery date approached, fear consumed me again – fear of the surgical procedure itself, the anesthesia, the potential complications. But this time, it was overshadowed by the even greater fear of the consequences of not having the surgery. The possibility of developing another PE, or eventually developing diabetes – a disease my son battled daily through no fault of his own – felt like constant threats. I couldn't bear the thought of potentially causing myself a disease Scott had no control over. The responsibility I felt towards him, towards being healthy for him and my other boys, solidified my determination. I had to face my fears and take control of my health.

In November 2019, I underwent a sleeve gastrectomy. Over the following year, I experienced substantial weight loss, shedding a total of 140 pounds. It felt transformative. But the surgery was far from an easy way out. The physical recovery involved significant pain, discomfort, and adjusting to a radically different way of eating. Mentally and emotionally, the challenges were immense. The persistent desire for food, the "head hunger," coupled with the physical inability to satisfy those cravings, created a constant internal conflict. Learning to nourish my body with tiny portions, dealing with vitamin deficiencies, navigating social situations centered around food – it was a daily struggle.

Going into the surgery, I hadn't believed I was permanently saying goodbye to my favorite foods. My initial plan, perhaps naive, was to lose the weight and then gradually reintroduce carbs and some sugar, adhering to an 80/20 rule of healthy eating versus occasional indulgences. I was convinced I could maintain the loss this way.

However, I eventually had to confront the reality of my relationship with food – it felt deeply ingrained, almost like an addiction, tied inextricably to comfort, stress, and reward. Furthermore, I recognized my unhealthy psychological attachment to my weight, viewing excess weight almost like a protective "security blanket."

I oscillated between wanting to feel attractive and confident, the "sexy wife" standing beside my handsome husband, and wanting to hide away, gain weight back, and subconsciously fear any sort of external attraction, perhaps as a defense mechanism against potential harm or betrayal.

My previous significant weight loss in 2011 had triggered insecurity in my ex-husband, and my own behavior then, reveling in the attention, wasn't something I was proud of.

Before this surgery, with Keith's support, I dedicated significant time to therapy, addressing these complex emotional issues – the fear of losing weight again, the fear it might negatively impact my relationship. It was only because of the profound difference I perceived in our relationship, the trust I had in Keith and in myself at that time, that I felt able to proceed.

Despite the surgery and initial success, maintaining the weight loss proved incredibly difficult over the next couple of years, just as it always had before.

The old patterns, the emotional eating, the psychological comfort of the "security blanket," began to creep back in, especially during times of stress like the pandemic layoff.

While I didn't regain all the weight, a significant portion returned, highlighting that the surgery addressed the physical capacity but not the deep-seated emotional and psychological drivers of my lifelong struggle with obesity.

It was during this period of re-gain and frustration, sometime in 2022, that I came across the book *Bright Line Eating*.

Reading it was another revelation. Learning about the science behind food addiction, how sugar impacts brain chemistry much like addictive drugs, and understanding that willpower is a finite resource, limited to perhaps only a few minutes per day against intense cravings, shifted my perspective dramatically. It helped me finally accept that my struggle wasn't just a lack of discipline; it was a complex interplay of biology, psychology, and likely, trauma responses.

This understanding allowed me to finally let go of the shame and accept that interventions like surgery or medication weren't the "easy way out," but potentially necessary tools for managing what felt like a genuine disease.

Recognizing that I needed a different, more sustainable approach, one that addressed the underlying biological and psychological factors beyond simple restriction or willpower, I began researching other options.

In October 2022, armed with this new understanding and acceptance, after discussions with my doctor about the ongoing challenges, I started taking a GLP-1 medication.

This approach felt fundamentally different. It wasn't just about restriction; it seemed to quiet the constant "food noise" in my brain, reduce cravings, and address some of the metabolic issues that likely contributed to my weight struggles. For the first time, it felt less like a constant battle of willpower against my own body and mind, and more like a partnership.

As of writing this update, I am currently at my lowest adult weight and have been successfully maintaining it for over two years. It feels like I have finally found a path that allows me to manage this aspect of my physical health in a sustainable way, freeing up precious energy to focus on continued emotional and mental healing.

The same resilience that carried me through career pivots, layoffs, and new opportunities is now rooted in my health — and for the first time, my body feels like it's on my side. That changes everything.

CHAPTER 28

(D)istance

Taking control of my physical health, finding a path that finally felt sustainable after decades of struggle, was a significant step forward. But true healing required more than just managing weight; it demanded confronting the deep-seated emotional wounds, particularly those related to family dynamics and the weight of the past. And I came to realize, perhaps counterintuitively, that confronting those wounds most effectively required perspective, which, for me, necessitated physical distance.

Family relationships are a paradox, capable of bringing immense joy and profound sorrow, often simultaneously. The longing for belonging, for a safe haven within our family of origin, is universal—a primal desire for unconditional love and acceptance from those who share our bloodline, regardless of our shortcomings or mistakes.

As a child, I yearned desperately for a father figure who was a protector, someone who would fiercely defend my innocence against any threat. Instead, my own father, grappling with his own complex loyalties, failed to fulfill that role in the face of his own father's betrayal, leaving a gaping wound.

Years passed, filled with fraught attempts to navigate the fractured landscape of our family. Moments of connection and genuine affection were inevitably interspersed with periods of painful distance, triggered by my attempts to speak about the past or his inability to hear it.

By 2017, I found myself still grappling with lingering questions, still needing understanding about his choices surrounding the abuse and its aftermath. After numerous failed attempts to communicate directly—where conversations inevitably dissolved into his anger or dismissiveness and my subsequent hurt withdrawal—I finally reached a breaking point.

Fueled more by years of frustration and simmering anger than by genuine hope for resolution, I poured my raw emotions into a letter. A small, perhaps foolish, part of me clung to the possibility that words on paper might elicit some acknowledgment or understanding.

I read an article today on intrafamilial sexual abuse. Curious as to how a parent should handle such devastating news. Of course, it confirmed everything that I have ever thought. That every child has a chance to heal but they NEED the support of parents, extended family, the community, and professionals.

I have tried to put myself in your shoes. And in that place, I know I would be heartbroken. I would be angry. I would be confused. I would feel like I failed as a parent. But I would 100% have my child's back. My dad, or whoever dared to harm my child in such a selfless, life-

altering manner, would be dead to me. Ironically here I am, feeling that my dad is just as dead as your dad actually is.

Nowhere in that article did I read that a parent's best course of action is to protect the pedophile. Nowhere did I read that the best course of action is to put a band aid on a severed artery and call it good. I may not have been literally bleeding out but your band aid of "here go see a therapist whether you want to or not" did NOTHING. And instead of acknowledging that at any time where I have tried to tell you I was hurt your answer has been "haven't we dealt with this shit already?!" You may have when you chose to sweep things under the rug. When you chose to go to court to protect your father. When you choose repeatedly to hold my words against me all the while telling me to let go of my own hurt. When you choose to allow me to feel less than and guilty and angry and HURT.

When someone tells us we have hurt them we don't get to decide that we didn't. We can ignore it. We can be defensive. We can project our own hurt and find justification. But we CANNOT decide for that person that we did not, in fact, hurt them.

My grandfather took something from me I can never get back, but my innocence has been the least of the damage. He took even more from me when his entire family minimalized the damage and over the years cared less and less as I hurt more and more. And what's worse is that any time I have tried to heal, to talk, to understand...I am just crazy and dramatic and not worth the effort. NOT WORTH THE EFFORT. I was not worth the effort it took to deal with the hurt head on, over 20 years ago and I am not worth the effort it would take now. I, YOUR daughter, am NOT WORTH THE EFFORT. Which in turn makes it IMPOSSIBLE for me to value myself the way one should.

I decided last year, after reaching out to some of your family and having my feelings dismissed, that I was done. That it was either keep trying to heal and understand and have those relationships I was so desperate for, or to let go. Knowing both would hurt, I was finally at a place where self-preservation determined my need to let go. And you were right there in that mix, but you were different. Letting go of the relationship I always wished I had...The one where my daddy held me and comforted me and told me everything was going to be alright, be it 10 or 36, meant missing out on time with some of the very few people I feel care about me in this world. And so, I tried. And now I am done.

You are my parent; I am your child. And as imperfect as I am, it was your responsibility to protect and love me unconditionally. I will no longer allow you to make me feel guilty for the way I have lived my life. For the way I have tried to heal or for the things I have done or said. No matter what I have ever said to you, you must know those words would NEVER have been spoken had you just been the dad I should have had. The dad I deserved.

The silence was its own loud answer, confirming the painful truth I had already begun to accept—the truth I likely expected when I sent the letter fueled by years of frustration.

I've made a concerted effort over the years to step outside my own perspective, to try and see things from his point of view, or the perspective of others in my family who seemed unable or unwilling to fully acknowledge the depth of the betrayal.

However, despite my best attempts at empathy, my own lived experiences inevitably cloud my judgment. While parts of me can perhaps understand the crushing weight of realizing your hero—your own father—is actually the villain, I will never be able to comprehend prioritizing anything above a child's safety and well-being when it comes to abuse. There is absolutely no situation where the abuser should ever be given precedence over the child.

The betrayal of trust, the emotional damage inflicted—these are immeasurable. A child's innocence and vulnerability must always be paramount, and any action or decision that fails to protect them from harm is, in my view, unconscionable.

Family remains a complex tapestry woven with threads of love, loyalty, shared history, and sometimes, profound hurt. The love I feel for my family is unwavering, fierce even, a bond forged in shared childhoods and undeniable connection. But the journey of life, particularly the journey of healing from trauma within a family system, has taught me that love and like, or love and approval, or love and healthy interaction, are not always intertwined.

As I've grown older, I've come to understand that love doesn't require blind acceptance or silence in the face of hurt. It's possible to love deeply while acknowledging differences, disagreements, and profound pain. True love, I believe, allows for honesty—for the expression of one's truth—even when that truth challenges the family narrative or causes discomfort.

Sometimes, love necessitates creating distance—not as a rejection of the people, but as an act of self-preservation, a way to maintain healthy boundaries needed for one's own survival and healing. It's an act of self-love to recognize when distance is necessary to protect our own well-being, even when it's painful and lonely to do so.

This need for distance became clearer, almost unavoidable, after Keith, William, and I made the significant move from Utah to Texas in 2021. Scott and Owen would follow us a year later, completing our family unit in this new state.

While I had initially been genuinely excited about relocating—eager to experience life outside the pervasive, often insular LDS culture of Utah County, hoping for a more diverse environment where Keith might face less overt or subtle racism, envisioning a true fresh start away from the ghosts of my past—the reality of the move proved incredibly difficult.

The emotional toll of being physically distant from my roots, my complicated but familiar support system, the mountains that felt like part of my soul, was far greater than I anticipated.

We purchased a beautiful home in a Texas suburb, complete with the sparkling blue inground swimming pool I had dreamed of my entire life—a tangible symbol, perhaps, of achieving a certain kind of middle-class stability and normalcy I had always craved.

The initial few months were a whirlwind of unpacking boxes, settling in, exploring our new surroundings under the vast Texas sky. Frequent work travel back to Utah during that time allowed me to see my boys (before they all moved down) and the rest of my family often enough to stave off severe homesickness, creating a buffer against the full impact of the relocation.

However, this idyllic period didn't last. As the seasons shifted and the humid Texas heat gave way to a surprisingly bleak winter, a profound sense of isolation began to creep in, insidious and heavy.

The once-inviting pool lay dormant under the chilly winter air, the water still, reflecting the gray sky—a stark reminder of the warmth and vibrancy that had vanished with the summer sun.

Shorter days and unexpectedly colder temperatures meant less time spent outdoors enjoying our new backyard, and more time confined indoors, amplifying the feelings of detachment from my loved ones back in Utah. The sheer distance felt immense, insurmountable some days.

Around this time, I had pushed myself physically, training harder than ever to complete a 10k run on my treadmill, achieving the goal with a surge of pride and exhilaration.

It felt good to accomplish something tangible, something difficult. But the victory was short-lived. The day after my 10k triumph, a nagging pain started deep in my foot, sharp and insistent with every step.

A doctor's visit confirmed heel spurs and plantar fasciitis, painful consequences of intense training on an aging body. This injury was a major setback, not just physically but mentally.

Unable to run or even swim comfortably in the now-chilly pool, my primary outlets for stress relief, physical activity, and feeling capable were suddenly gone.

The combination of forced inactivity, the frustration of the injury, and the growing sense of geographic and emotional isolation took a heavy toll. The weight I had worked so hard to keep off began to creep back on, and I fell into a deep, suffocating depression, the familiar darkness settling over me once again.

Was I ever going to escape this cycle? Would I ever truly feel whole?

It was during this difficult period—confined indoors by weather and injury, struggling both physically and emotionally, feeling isolated and adrift in my new Texas life—that I threw myself fully into this project: the writing of this book.

Pouring the stories out, revisiting the painful memories, trying to make sense of the chaos on the page became my primary focus, my therapy, my reason for getting out of bed some days.

As I delved deeper into the past, forcing myself to confront the memories and emotions I had perhaps kept at bay for years through sheer busyness or the constant low-grade drama of proximity to family, I had a stark realization: there was absolutely no way I could have undertaken this level of emotional excavation, this raw, unflinching confrontation with my past, if I were still living in Utah.

There, every attempt to heal, every effort to process the emotional wounds, had felt fraught, inevitably bumping up against the resistance, dismissal, or lack of support from key family members.

The frustration and hurt would become overwhelming, inevitably leading me to cut off contact—with my dad, a sister, sometimes the entire family—for periods of time, creating more drama and pain.

The isolation during those times was acute, agonizing. Missing family gatherings, spending holidays alone in my bedroom, consumed by tears and sadness—the emotional pain felt unbearable.

Eventually, desperate for connection, I would find a way to bury the hurt again, often by organizing a social event or finding some other excuse to bring everyone back together, smoothing things over, perpetuating the cycle of silence and superficial harmony.

Creating physical distance by moving to Texas, while initially difficult and triggering its own form of isolation, had inadvertently created the necessary emotional space.

The hundreds of miles provided a crucial buffer, allowing me to engage with the trauma on my own terms, without the immediate pressure of family reactions, opinions, or the ingrained patterns of interaction that often left me feeling silenced or invalidated.

This distance—this separation from the environment where so much hurt had occurred and been subsequently minimized or denied—was, I realized with clarity, a crucial, necessary step for my own well-being and for the possibility of genuine, lasting healing.

It was in this quiet, sometimes lonely space, paradoxically created by physical distance, that I could finally begin to truly confront the past, wrestle with its complexities, and prepare to share my story—unfiltered and whole.

CHAPTER 29

(H)ealing

Achieving career success, traveling the world, experiencing moments of pure joy like the one on the beach with my family—these were tangible signs that my life was moving forward, that I was finding my footing after years of struggle. Yet, beneath the surface of these accomplishments, the invisible wounds of the past continued to exert their influence in ways I was only beginning to understand. Healing wasn't just about external success; it required confronting the internal landscape I had long tried to ignore or power through. And a core part of that landscape was my relationship with my own mental health.

For years, I avoided even using those words—mental health—about myself. I had seen too many survivors have their credibility dismantled simply because someone labeled them with a diagnosis. It's one of the most effective tactics for silencing victims of sexual abuse: suggest they're "unstable," and suddenly every truth they speak is called into question. I refused to give anyone that weapon against me.

Instead, I clung to a different identity: I was never a victim, I was always a survivor. And survivors, in my mind, didn't talk about anxiety or depression. They powered through. They didn't give anyone an excuse to say, *See? She's just unstable.* I wore my silence like armor, convinced it made me strong.

The truth, though, is that I'd had anxiety for as long as I can remember. I just didn't know what to call it. I had coping mechanisms—numbing, overworking, throwing myself into chaos— that looked like rebellion from the outside but were really survival tactics on the inside. I'd learned to live with a constant hum of tension, to normalize self-destructive patterns, and to convince myself they were personality quirks instead of trauma responses.

For years, I told myself that naming any mental health struggle would make me weak. The irony, of course, is that refusing to name them made me weaker. Denial didn't erase the anxiety, depression, and intrusive thoughts—it just meant I carried them alone, without tools or support.

Following the robbery when I was eighteen, and after years spent perpetuating that web of deceit, I reached a turning point: a resolute commitment to truth-telling, regardless of embarrassment or legal repercussions. I decided I would own my shit—a mantra that became my personal compass. While that sounded empowering, it was also another way of overcompensating, still rooted in the belief that I was inherently flawed and had to constantly prove otherwise.

By 2019, despite all the outward successes, I felt stuck. That's when I returned to therapy, determined to finally fix whatever was holding me back. My therapist suggested EMDR (eye movement desensitization and reprocessing). She explained that by following her moving pencil back and forth with my eyes, I could begin to reprocess stuck memories, shifting them from the reactive, emotional part of my brain into the narrative part where they could be integrated.

I was skeptical—my only frame of reference was a failed attempt at hypnotism years earlier that felt silly and ineffective—but I was desperate enough to try.

At first, the process seemed mechanical. I followed the pencil, talked about random things, doubted anything was happening. But near the end of that first session, when I focused on a painful memory, tears began streaming down my face without warning.

Weeks later my therapist and I agreed I'd made progress. Certain triggers didn't feel as sharp. I felt lighter. I was healed! Or so I thought.

I wasn't. Not fully. EMDR helped process specific memories, but I realized there was a crucial piece missing: self-forgiveness. I could acknowledge my growth, but I still carried shame. I still judged myself for the ways I'd acted in survival mode.

That's when I started reading—everything I could get my hands on about trauma. I devoured memoirs like K.L. Randis's *Spilled Milk*, feeling less alone in my experiences. I studied Bessel van der Kolk's *The Body Keeps the Score*, where I learned how trauma physically changes brain chemistry and shapes behavior. That understanding changed everything. My choices weren't proof of inherent badness—they were the brain and body's adaptations to extreme stress.

I also explored Internal Family Systems through Richard Schwartz's *No Bad Parts*, where I learned to meet my younger selves—the scared little girl, the furious teenager—with compassion instead of contempt. These weren't "crazy" parts of me. They were hurt parts, and they'd been protecting me the only ways they knew how.

It became clear: my anxiety, depression, PTSD—they weren't signs that I was broken. They were evidence that I had endured. And the same labels once used to discredit survivors? I would now claim them as proof of survival, not shame.

My abuse doesn't define me, but it has undeniably shaped me—in every complex, challenging, and imperfect way. Acknowledging that impact isn't about excusing mistakes; it's about understanding their origins and taking responsibility for my healing. I believe in accountability with every fiber of my being, but it's impossible to ignore how profoundly sexual abuse and trauma shape the way we think, feel, and act. Trauma rewires the brain and body, distorting perception, clouding judgment, and pushing us toward coping mechanisms—like dissociation or hypervigilance—that can be as destructive as they are protective. For me, one of the most disruptive was the sudden onset of anxiety attacks.

The first anxiety attack I can clearly name happened years earlier, just after I escaped a toxic relationship following my divorce from Eric. I went to my parents' house expecting refuge, but safety turned to battle within minutes. My brother, reacting to my defense against his wife's cutting remark, unleashed years of unspoken resentment. His words hit like blows. Fear and fury surged through me—hot, dizzying, impossible to contain.

In an instant, fight or flight took over. I hurled my keys and phone across the room, desperate to release the energy raging inside me. When they finally left, the adrenaline crashed. I collapsed on the floor, sobbing, my body curling tight as my hands and feet tingled, locked, and convulsed. I didn't know it then, but that was my first full-blown anxiety attack—a moment when my nervous system, already shaped by years of trauma, could no longer hold the weight without breaking.

From then on, anxiety attacks became an unwelcome shadow. Sometimes I could feel them stalking me—too much noise, too many demands, one sharp comment too many. Other times they struck without warning, a storm I couldn't outrun. The fear of having an attack began to shape my choices as much as the attacks themselves.

When I was at the hospital for the rape exam, the victim's advocate handed me a card for the Rape Recovery Center. I tucked it away without making the call. I wasn't ready—not yet.

A week later, I was sitting in a jail cell. That was my rock bottom. Lower than the rape. Lower than anything I had ever felt. Stripped of control, safety, and dignity, I knew something had to change. This time, I couldn't ignore the lifeline I'd been given.

When I was released, I pulled out that card. This time, I didn't push it aside. I knew I needed help.

It would be the first time I had ever chosen therapy as an adult. The last time I'd been in a therapist's office, I was a teenager—forced into it by my parents, silent and unwilling. This time, I walked in on my own. I was desperate to be heard.

During intake, I feared being turned away because of the pending domestic violence charge from the week before. Through tears, I pleaded for them to see me as I was—not as a case file or a charge—but as a woman desperate for help. They made an exception.

In one session, when I felt the familiar swell of panic begin to rise, my therapist guided me into a visualization—my "happy place" on the softball field. I could smell the dirt, hear the crack of the bat, feel the sting of the ball in my glove. I stayed there in my mind, breathing in the calm, until the pressure in my chest eased and my heartbeat slowed. Panic didn't win that day.

Over the next several years, I didn't "cure" my anxiety, but I learned how to live with it. I stumbled at times—slipping back into unhealthy coping, letting stress pile until it cracked me open—but each return to the tools I'd learned made the recovery a little faster, a little steadier. Therapy had planted seeds I didn't even realize were growing until I found myself responding differently to challenges that once would have broken me.

By the time my oldest son, Scott, was a young adult, I'd come to see mental health as something you don't "fix" once—it's something you tend to for life. That perspective became even more important in December 2021, when Scott was diagnosed with bipolar disorder, generalized anxiety disorder, depression, and attention deficit disorder. None of it was a surprise, but the weight of those words still landed heavy. He already lived with more than his fair share of physical illness. Now this.

Watching him navigate his mental health has been like holding up a mirror to my own journey. When he feels worthless, I remind him—firmly—that he is not his diagnoses. That his struggle isn't weakness. That showing up each day under the weight he carries is a form of strength most people will never understand.

His battle has sharpened my conviction: mental health conditions are not character flaws. They are as real and worthy of care as a broken bone or a chronic disease. We wouldn't tell someone with a cast to "just get over it." We shouldn't do it to those with invisible wounds either.

I used to believe that acknowledging my mental health would make me less credible. Now I know the opposite is true. Speaking it aloud is a refusal to be silenced—especially when it's the part of the story someone else might try to use against me.

CHAPTER 30

(B)ias

In March 2022, I took a leap that felt equal parts terrifying and right. I reached out directly to our CEO with an idea: I wanted to join a colleague who was teaching Linux and life skills at his daughter's high school—not to teach tech, but to speak with students about resilience, self-worth, and navigating life after trauma. It wasn't the kind of conversation anyone expected from someone in my role, but that was exactly the point.

She responded with encouragement and connected me with our Chief Communications Officer, who agreed it was worth pursuing. The plan began to take shape, and I threw myself into preparing. I didn't want to just "show up and speak." I wanted to connect. I wanted to give those students something real—something I wish someone had given me at their age.

But in the middle of that preparation, another opportunity emerged. I was invited to speak to our company's Women in Tech group as part of our March Breaking the Bias event. Not only would my colleagues be in the audience, but I was given the option to open the invite to anyone in my personal life. That meant my friends, my extended family, even my parents could attend.

This would be the first time my family had ever been willing to hear me. And the reason it worked was because it wasn't a back-and-forth conversation; it was me speaking. I could say what needed to be said without being interrupted, talked over, or dismissed. That alone felt monumental.

The months leading up to the presentation became a period of relentless self-questioning and emotional excavation. Each day, I grappled with overwhelming stress and anxiety, which manifested physically in a cascade of ailments: constant diarrhea, bone-deep fatigue, throbbing tension headaches, the incessant ringing of tinnitus, a sinus infection that lingered despite antibiotics, a back that seized so suddenly it left me bedridden for over a week, and an alarming fifty-pound weight gain despite my earlier success. My body was screaming under the strain of the internal conflict.

The period preceding the presentation was also filled with an overwhelming, paradoxical sadness. My life, objectively, was filled with countless blessings—a loving husband in Keith, wonderful children growing into young men, a successful and fulfilling career, financial stability, a beautiful home.

Yet, this deep well of sorrow persisted. The incongruity fueled my anger and frustration. *Why can't I just be happy? What is wrong with me?*

It prompted an urgent call to my therapist. Despite the undeniable benefits therapy had provided over the years, a part of me remained skeptical—surely, I've already processed everything?

As she had done countless times before, she listened patiently and then offered an insight that hit me with the force of truth.

Her words struck a chord: "Chaos is your comfort zone."

She explained that when life flowed smoothly—when things were calm and stable—my brain, conditioned by decades of trauma and turmoil, unconsciously gravitated toward self-destructive behaviors or harmful habits. Stability felt foreign, uncomfortable, almost boring.

Years of internalized worthlessness had shaped my reality; it made a strange kind of psychological sense that a fulfilling marriage and a successful career would leave me feeling adrift.

While her explanation resonated intellectually, making logical sense of my persistent unease, a part of me still resisted—could it really be that simple? Was I truly sabotaging my own happiness?

I found myself lying awake at night, wondering why anyone would willingly subject themselves to this kind of torment just to tell a story. Was it worth it?

Yet that same inner voice that once urged me to apply for the tech job answered with certainty: *yes*. On the other side of the fear and the physical symptoms was a profound sense of peace—of integration—that I could not reach without walking through this fire.

The anxiety wasn't just about sharing vulnerability with colleagues or strangers. It was about my family—especially my dad. My attempts to have open, honest conversations with him about the past had always been met with anger, defensiveness, or silence. I loved him deeply, but resentment had lived beside that love for years. I knew that exposing the betrayal in his actions during court would wound him, perhaps humiliate him. It would hurt my mom, the kindest soul I know, forcing her to confront truths she'd avoided. And my grandmother, who had already carried so much shame because of her ex-husband, would feel the weight too.

All of this sat heavy on me. And still, that inner voice insisted: *You have to share your story.*

I remembered a quote I'd saved years ago: "We are not required to set ourselves on fire to keep other people warm." For decades, I had done the opposite, burning myself out to protect others—especially my family. But this time, I wasn't going to.

The day before the presentation, the anxiety reached a fever pitch. My stomach was in knots, my thoughts racing. I felt an intense, almost overwhelming urge to connect with my dad, despite the history of failed conversations. He knew I was writing my story, preparing to share something personal at work, but we hadn't discussed the specifics. I didn't want a conversation. I simply needed him to hear me, just once, before I stepped onto that virtual stage.

When he answered the phone, his familiar, "Hello?" sounded normal, unsuspecting. Through tears that were already flowing, I explained, "Dad, I don't want to talk, I just need to say something, and then I'm going to hang up."

Confused, he listened as I choked out, "I love you."

His own voice thick with sudden emotion, he replied, "Wow, Amber, I wasn't expecting that."

I pressed on quickly, the difficult words tumbling out before I lost my nerve. "But what I have to say tomorrow is going to hurt you." Then I hung up.

Almost instantly, he texted, "Why did you hang up?"

"That's what I wanted to say," I typed back, my thumbs trembling. "That I love you. I don't want to hurt you, but I am hurt, and I can't tell my story without addressing that pain. I just need you to know that I love you."

He seemed confused, replying simply that I hadn't actually said anything substantial. I responded, "I have, and I will continue to do so as I write and share my story. Not to you personally, but to the world. I don't want to force a conversation or change our relationship. I just cannot embark on this journey without first telling you that hurting you or anyone else is far from my intention."

His simple, two-letter reply—"Ok"—stung with its curtness, its lack of warmth or understanding. Even though I wasn't expecting absolution, it felt like another small dismissal, a reminder of the void between us.

CHAPTER 31

The morning of the presentation, my stomach churned as if I'd swallowed a hive of angry bees. I sat at my desk, camera off, headset waiting, cursor hovering over the "Join meeting" button. Somewhere on the other side of that link, my colleagues were logging in—some I worked with daily, others I'd never met. And for the first time, the audience also included people from my personal life. My mom. My dad. Friends. Extended family. People who had lived through parts of this story with me, and others who had only ever seen the polished, professional version of me.

There was no turning back.

I took a deep breath, clicked "Join", and the familiar company logo appeared on the screen. My name was introduced, the event framed as part of our Breaking the Bias series, and suddenly the small green light above my webcam flicked on—my silent cue that it was time.

The words I had practiced tumbled out in the order I'd rehearsed, but they no longer felt rehearsed. They felt lived. I spoke about mental health stigma. About resilience. About the biases—internal and external—that keep people silent. And then, I told the truth. My truth. The abuse. The arrests. The shame. The journey through chaos into something like stability.

It was not a conversation; it was me claiming my space and my voice.

In that moment, I wasn't just speaking to my colleagues—I was speaking to my family without their ability to interrupt, deflect, or rewrite my story. I was speaking to the younger version of myself who had needed someone to model what survival and healing could look like.

When I finished, the virtual applause came in the form of chat messages. Words like brave, powerful, and needed. Some from colleagues I knew well. Some from names I didn't recognize. And tucked among them were the names of people I loved—my mom, my sister, my friends—leaving messages that made my throat tighten.

I didn't see a message from my dad.

After the call ended, I sat there, staring at the now-empty meeting screen. The adrenaline drained out of me, replaced by a stillness I hadn't anticipated. I had expected to feel relief, maybe even pride. Instead, I felt... different. Lighter, yes, but also profoundly aware that I had crossed a threshold. There was no taking the words back. My story was no longer something I carried in private—it was out there, living in the minds of dozens of people.

Within hours, private messages began to trickle in. Coworkers I barely knew thanked me for "putting words to things they'd never said out loud." Some shared their own histories of abuse, mental health struggles, and loss. One colleague told me she had never disclosed her assault to anyone outside of the closest people in her life before that day. Another said my talk gave her the courage to ask for a mental health accommodation at work.

Every message was a reminder: when one person speaks, it gives others permission to do the same.

In the weeks that followed, something unexpected happened. The conversation didn't fade—it deepened. People kept coming to me, sometimes in private messages late at night. They weren't asking me for solutions. They just wanted to be heard.

That's when the idea struck me: what if we created a dedicated space for this? A place where employees could share stories about the hard things—the things we usually keep out of workplace conversations—not for sympathy, but for understanding.

I called it Share Your Story.

The premise was simple: one person would volunteer to share a deeply personal life experience—anything from abuse, to war, to cancer, divorce, or neurodivergence—while others simply listened. It wasn't about debating, fixing, or offering platitudes. It was about holding space.

Our first session was quiet, but powerful. People spoke with a rawness that made their stories linger in the room long after they stopped talking. Some shared through tears. Others spoke with steady voices that somehow carried even more weight. Every single one expanded our capacity for compassion.

The stories didn't just stay in the room—they reshaped the fabric of how we worked together. What began as individual acts of courage grew into a culture where vulnerability became strength and community could truly flourish. As our global HR executive later reflected, "Amber created a space where vulnerability became strength and where community could flourish in incredible ways. I've seen firsthand how deeply this initiative touched people and transformed our culture." Leaders became more intentional in how they supported their teams, quiet voices stepped forward with new initiatives, and people began using words like safe, understood, and connected to describe our workplace.

I realized then that what had happened during my Breaking the Bias talk wasn't just a personal milestone—it was the spark for something bigger. Speaking my truth had given other people the courage to speak theirs. And together, we were changing the culture of our workplace, one story at a time.

What I didn't fully grasp then was that Share Your Story was only the beginning. Creating space for honesty and compassion at work had shown me what was possible—and it planted the seed for what I would later take far beyond SUSE. The same courage it took to speak there would carry me into rooms, stages, and conversations I once thought were impossible.

CHAPTER 32

(R)estitution

Sharing my story at work felt like a monumental step, a significant moment of breaking the silence and claiming my truth. The outpouring of support was validating, and for the first time, I felt truly seen in my struggle—not just as a competent professional, but as a whole person with a complex past. Yet, even as I celebrated this victory, this new level of openness, the journey was far from over. The presentation had cracked open the door to deeper healing, but I knew, with a certainty that settled in my bones, that I needed more than weekly therapy sessions to truly address the decades of complex trauma that still echoed within me. Life felt good on the surface—career success, a marriage to Keith that felt supportive and loving—but the internal pain persisted, a constant, low hum of anxiety and unresolved grief beneath it all.

I began researching intensive healing options, spending hours online, my search terms a litany of my needs: trauma retreats, childhood sexual abuse recovery programs, intensive therapy for PTSD. I figured there must be something akin to rehab for addiction, but focused on survivors—a dedicated space for profound healing.

The websites I found were filled with images of serene landscapes, testimonials of transformation, and descriptions of therapeutic modalities I'd only vaguely heard of. Hope flickered, but it was quickly tempered by reality. The costs were daunting, often tens of thousands of dollars for a week or two of specialized care—amounts that felt completely out of reach. A cruel irony: the very healing I desperately needed seemed reserved for those with significant financial resources. The weight of that financial barrier felt like another form of injustice.

It was during this period of actively seeking deeper healing resources—feeling both hopeful about the possibilities and despairing about the cost—that news arrived of my grandfather's second wife's death. I don't recall how I heard—a phone call, a text from a family member. My immediate reaction was a complicated numbness, followed by a strange, almost detached wave of finality. Any faint, lingering, perhaps childish hope that my grandfather might have left something behind—a letter of apology tucked away, a small financial provision in his will passed through her, some acknowledgment intended to try and fix even a fraction of what he broke—vanished completely with her passing.

Word eventually confirmed what I already suspected: the inheritance from my grandfather's estate, now fully accessible, would be split among his four children (my father and his siblings) and his late wife's four children. There was, of course, nothing designated for me—the grandchild whose life he had irrevocably damaged. This felt like the final dismissal from him, the ultimate proof that accountability, even posthumously, was not forthcoming from that branch of the family.

Knowing this, and feeling the urgency of my own need for intensive treatment, I decided I had to confront the issue of restitution directly with my family. It wasn't just about the money for a retreat; it was about acknowledgment—about them, his children, making right what he never did. I contacted my parents, expressing my fear that if I didn't get specialized help soon, the cumulative stress could seriously impact my already fragile health, or worse.

I texted my dad first, my thumbs shaking slightly as I typed out the difficult question, asking if any portion of my grandfather's estate, would be directed to me as a form of restitution. I already knew the answer, a cold certainty in my gut, but I needed to ask—to hear it. As expected, he said no. He then added, in a tone that felt matter-of-fact even through text, that my siblings and I would need to wait until he and my mom passed away to receive our inheritance from them—a completely separate issue that felt like a deflection.

The response, though anticipated, still felt cold, dismissive of the unique, specific financial and emotional burden my grandfather's actions had placed directly on me throughout my life. I pressed further, trying to make him understand the distinction. I asked if there had been any consideration among him and his sisters—my grandfather's direct heirs—to allocate a portion of their inheritance from him as restitution to me, the person he had directly harmed. His reply was a brief, unequivocal, and stern "no". No explanation, no discussion, just a closed door.

Trying a different angle, hoping to appeal to his sense of reason or fairness, I sent him an article I'd found detailing the estimated lifetime financial impact of childhood sexual abuse—a staggering $300,000 average, encompassing therapy costs, lost income, medical bills related to trauma, and more. I asked if he knew this. He said he did not. I asked if he felt my grandfather should have been financially responsible for the damage he did. After a pause, my dad conceded that when he was alive, my grandfather "should have owned up to a lot of stuff."

A small, almost insignificant admission, yet it felt like something. I agreed, then stated plainly my belief: that his father's money, the inheritance they were now receiving, should have, in an ideal world, gone to me to cover the costs of healing. That my grandfather should have made that provision. But since he hadn't, they—his children—now had the opportunity, perhaps the moral obligation, to make it right. I was asking him, his son, to do what his father had so profoundly failed to do.

His response remained unchanged: I would have to wait with my siblings for our inheritance. The conversation was over in his mind.

The finality of his refusal—the complete unwillingness to acknowledge a direct financial responsibility tied to the harm caused by his father—felt like another profound betrayal, echoing his actions in the courtroom decades earlier when he pleaded for mercy for his father instead of justice for me. It wasn't just about the money for the retreat; it was about the principle, about accountability, about acknowledging the specific, lasting damage inflicted upon me, damage with tangible financial consequences.

It was then, feeling a potent mixture of desperation, anger, and a lifetime of accumulated hurt, that I sent the following text to both of my parents: "I need treatment, now, before the stress makes me any sicker than I already am, or worse, kills me. I don't give a shit if anyone thinks I am being dramatic. I'm tired of suffering so that the rest of the family doesn't have to. If you're not willing to step up and cover restitution, I need you to pay for treatment. This is not my fault. I couldn't advocate for myself when I was a child. That was your job and you both failed me. Don't keep failing me. Please stop failing me."

My dad's reply was brief and, to me, utterly dismissive of the depth of my plea: he hoped I did get treatment, and that I had insurance for that. *Insurance.* His response echoed a familiar theme from my childhood; back then, his way of "helping" me after the abuse came to light was to send me to therapy. The underlying message always felt like a therapist would "fix" me, as if I were the sole problem, the only one in the family needing professional intervention. Now, years later, the suggestion of insurance felt like a similar deflection, a way of placing the responsibility for healing solely on my shoulders—as if standard health insurance would cover the intensive, specialized trauma retreats I was looking at, or undo decades of damage.

Just weeks before this painful exchange, shortly after my work presentation—which my parents and siblings had all tuned in for—I had received a surprising, hope-inducing text from my dad. He said he'd been watching a movie, and a scene had caused him to think of me. He wrote that he realized at that moment that his little girl had needed help, and for the first time ever, he apologized for his past failures to protect me.

It was something I had waited my entire life to hear, a moment that brought tears of relief and a fragile sense of hope. Overwhelmed, I immediately responded that I forgave him, that I loved him. In that moment, it truly felt like a breakthrough—like we were finally moving forward, that perhaps he finally understood the depth of my pain and his role in it.

Now, only months later, faced with my desperate plea for tangible help directly related to the consequences of his father's actions, that apology felt hollow—like empty words. The door that had seemed to crack open, offering a glimpse of potential healing and reconciliation, slammed shut again with a resounding thud. His suggestion that insurance should cover intensive trauma treatment felt like another deflection, minimizing the extraordinary nature of the healing required, and abdicating any familial responsibility.

The message was clear: emotional acknowledgment in a text message was one thing, but tangible restitution or active support for the deep healing I so desperately needed was off the table.

Beyond angry and hurt, feeling utterly abandoned in my pursuit of healing, I made a decision fueled by years of frustration and a lifetime of feeling silenced and unseen. I posted about the exchange— about the denial of help—on my Facebook page. It was an impulsive act, born of pain and a desire to be heard, to expose what felt like a profound injustice.

The reaction was swift, but not in the form of the support or understanding I craved. My youngest sister attacked me publicly in the comments, accusing me of trying to "out Dad," of making it sound like he'd done nothing but hurt me, of telling the world how "evil" he was and how unsupported I felt by the entire family. She declared I had "crossed the line."

The familiar pattern repeated itself with sickening predictability: speak the uncomfortable truth, challenge the family narrative, and be labeled the problem—the one causing drama, the ungrateful child.

The contrast between my father's apology after the presentation and his refusal to help financially after my grandfather's widow's death was jarring. It solidified the painful realization that despite any fleeting moments of perceived progress, when push came to shove, I would likely forever be left to heal on my own—responsible for picking up the pieces of a life shattered by actions that were never my fault.

The hurt intensified when I learned that my parents and one of my sisters had attended the funeral of my grandfather's second wife. Their presence there—paying respects to the woman who had, in my view, enabled my grandfather by her willful ignorance—felt like a profound minimization of my own experiences.

When I expressed my pain over their attendance, my youngest sister's response cut deep. She said something to the effect of, "We just can't win with you," implying my need for them to acknowledge my pain and make choices that reflected that understanding was unreasonable.

It felt like she was saying that if they couldn't support me on their terms—which included maintaining relationships I found harmful or invalidating—then a relationship with me was impossible.

In that moment, weary to my bones and raw with fresh grief, I told her she was right. I couldn't keep compromising my healing for their comfort—for their desire to maintain a facade of family unity that didn't include my truth.

I cut contact with everyone involved for several weeks, needing space to process the fresh layer of hurt, to lick my wounds, and to reaffirm my own boundaries, however lonely that path might be.

Chapter 33

(S)aprea

The painful dead end with my family regarding support for deeper healing, culminating in my decision to cut contact for several weeks, left me feeling raw and more isolated, but also strangely determined. If healing and understanding weren't going to come from within those familiar, fractured bonds, I would have to forge new paths and find sanctuary elsewhere.

I created TikTok and Instagram accounts, dedicating them to sharing my story, connecting with other survivors, and processing my experiences publicly. It felt empowering—a way to reclaim my narrative on my own terms, to find a community that did understand, even if it was virtual.

Around this time, the miniseries *Under the Banner of Heaven* premiered. Watching it, and later reading Jon Krakauer's book at my brother's suggestion, unearthed another layer of trauma I hadn't fully confronted. The series and book explored the roots of Mormonism—

including the early church's history of violence, patriarchal control, and emphasis on unquestioning obedience. Despite being raised in the mainstream LDS church, much of this history was new to me—or had been minimized. The realization that the faith of my upbringing was built on such disturbing origins felt like discovering I had been raised inside something far more controlling than I'd understood. Disgust, confusion, and a strange sense of betrayal swirled within me.

Seeking community and understanding for this new layer of disillusionment, I immersed myself in the online ex-Mormon community. It was there, amidst shared stories of deconstruction, religious trauma, and healing, that I connected with a fellow survivor—someone who understood both the religious trauma and the specific pain of childhood sexual abuse. Her messages were a lifeline.

It was she who first told me about Saprea, an organization offering healing retreats specifically for adult female survivors of childhood sexual abuse. She had attended their retreat and found it incredibly, profoundly healing.

Hope, fragile but persistent, sparked within me. But caution, born of past disappointments, followed closely. I immediately went to their website and applied, but I also researched the organization thoroughly. Discovering it was founded in Utah immediately raised red flags—was it connected to the LDS church? Would the retreat be filled with religious undertones that would be triggering rather than healing for someone like me, now grappling with religious trauma?

Saprea offered retreats in two locations at the time: Georgia and Utah. Knowing with every fiber of my being that I couldn't pursue this kind of deep, vulnerable healing anywhere near the geographical and emotional center of my past trauma, I opted for Georgia. I contacted Saprea via email, expressing my concerns about potential religious content. They responded quickly and compassionately, assuring me their healing programs were entirely secular, with no mention of religion. Reassured, my heart a little lighter, I finalized my plans, arranging flights and time off work.

The Saprea retreat in Georgia was, without exaggeration, one of the hardest yet most profoundly rewarding things I have ever done for myself. The retreat center was nestled in a quiet, wooded area, the air smelling of pine and damp earth. The first day was thick with an almost palpable anxiety. Seven other women, strangers from all walks of life, ranging in age from their early twenties to their sixties, gathered in the common room, our faces etched with a similar mixture of apprehension and fragile hope. We all carried the invisible weight of similar trauma, all unsure of what to expect, perhaps all wondering if this, finally, would be a place of true safety and understanding. The silence was heavy at first, broken only by the gentle voices of the facilitators.

But as we began, tentatively at first, to open up, to share our individual journeys—the raw details, the hidden shame, the lingering pain—a powerful realization dawned on each of us: for the first time ever, we were not alone. We were surrounded by women who understood without needing lengthy explanations, who saw the pain behind the carefully constructed smiles, who recognized the subtle language of survival in a shared glance or a knowing nod. There were tears, so many tears, but also, surprisingly, laughter—the gallows humor of survivors, the relief of shared experience.

Over the course of that intense week, through expertly facilitated support group sessions, educational workshops about trauma's impact on the brain and body, expressive arts activities, and moments of quiet reflection, an unbreakable sisterhood formed. We learned about trauma responses, about coping mechanisms, about shame and self-compassion. We laughed until our sides hurt, we cried until we were exhausted, we raged at the injustice of it all, and most importantly, we held space for each other's pain without judgment, without trying to fix—just witnessing and validating.

To this day, the eight of us maintain a group text thread—a lifeline where we check in, share hardships, celebrate victories, offer encouragement, and send love across the miles. These women, bound by shared experience and a fierce commitment to healing, became a chosen family, a sanctuary.

I returned home from Saprea feeling lighter, stronger, and fundamentally changed. The world looked brighter, colors seemed more vibrant. I remember a specific moment shortly after returning, just going about a normal day, tidying up in my kitchen, the Texas sun streaming through the window, this profound thought washed over me with absolute clarity, a wave of peaceful certainty: *I had made it.*

I could finally see the light at the end of the long, dark tunnel. The path ahead wouldn't be without challenges, I knew that, but the crushing weight of the past, the constant feeling of being broken and defined by my trauma, felt significantly lessened. It was replaced by a genuine, hopeful excitement for the future—for the possibilities that lay ahead now that I was equipped with new tools, a deeper understanding of myself, and the unwavering support of my Saprea sisters.

During those quiet days after the retreat, something else shifted. A poem I had started months earlier—lines that came from a place of pain but had remained unfinished—finally found its voice. The rest of it came effortlessly, as if my soul had been waiting for that retreat to open the floodgates. I wrote it for every version of me who needed to be seen. And I share it now—for every survivor still finding their voice.

The Sacrificial Lamb

I once was a little lamb
Whose hair was dark as night
My parents forced the church on me and
Told me "choose the right"

Don't fear my precious little lamb
For God is love and light
He knows your heart and hears your prayers
He'll always hold you tight

With tear-stained cheeks I bow my head
And plead with all my might
The monster under my bed is real
Please help me win this fight

The little lamb was sacrificed
Her innocence no more
"She'll be ok," her family said
"She chose this life," they swore

As she grows, that little lamb
>Becomes the blackest sheep
>She's a lost cause, they sigh in despair
>She's dug that hole too deep

No one would save her but herself
>As she wept her way to sleep
>She knew the battle up ahead
>Was long, and slow, and steep

They say what doesn't kill you
>Only makes you stronger
>I say my trauma doesn't get
>To take that credit any longer

With sheer determination
>To take back the life he stole
>She clawed and she climbed
>Until she emerged her true self—whole.

And then, just weeks later, when I was feeling more hopeful and whole than I had in years, life went boom. Again.

CHAPTER 34

(B)oom

December 2nd, 2022. It was a Friday morning, the air in the house still cool from the night. I had gone into Owen's room to wake him up for school. Sunlight was just beginning to peek through his blinds, casting striped shadows across his bed, but Owen was already wide awake, his eyes open in the dim light, looking like he might have been awake all night.

The air in his room felt heavy, charged with an unspoken tension. He looked at me, his face pale and visibly upset, his expression far too serious, too troubled for his age.

"Mom," his voice shaking, "I have to tell you something."

My heart gave a strange lurch. In those few seconds between him saying that and me managing to ask, "What is it? What's going on?" my mind raced through a horrifying Rolodex of possibilities. Had somebody died? Had something happened to one of his brothers? Something at school?

And then the words came out, quiet but each one landing like a physical blow, devastating in their simplicity:

"I think Keith's cheating on you."

In that instant, I knew he was right. There was no doubt, no room for denial. It was like a key turning in a lock, connecting scattered, previously dismissed observations. A moment about two weeks prior flashed in my mind: standing in the kitchen, frozen by a sudden, intrusive thought—*Is Keith cheating?* I had gotten angry with myself then, quickly dismissing it as paranoia, insecurity resurfacing. But the thought hadn't come from nowhere.

It had stemmed from small changes I'd noticed but hadn't allowed myself to consciously process: him spending more time tinkering in the garage, seemingly needing space; buying me puzzle after puzzle, perhaps as a distraction or peace offering; a strange comment he made about a song playing, asking if I was getting ready to leave him. Now, hearing my son voice the suspicion, those disparate pieces clicked into a horrifyingly clear picture. Keith was cheating. The light I thought I'd seen after Saprea was instantly, brutally extinguished.

Just days before this earth-shattering revelation, a seemingly innocent moment replayed in my mind with cruel irony. We had been in our living room, the evening light soft, and Taylor Swift's *Enchanted* started playing. We danced together, slowly, him holding me close. I remember focusing on the lyrics, "I was enchanted to meet you," feeling that sentiment so deeply, telling him how lucky I felt to have him in my life, how much I loved him. He had echoed the feelings, holding me tighter, telling me the same.

The other, more poignant line of the song—"Please don't be in love with someone else"—didn't even register then, completely overshadowed by the romantic haze I was in, by my belief in us. Now, that line screamed in my memory.

Adrenaline surged. I immediately went into action mode. Survival instinct, honed over years of crisis, took over. There was no room for tears yet, no space for the crushing weight of heartbreak to settle. First, action. I found a lawyer. I called my realtor. I gathered my other two sons, Scott and William, their faces etched with confusion and concern, and told them what Owen had discovered, the words feeling like stones in my mouth.

Scott, who had never fully settled into Texas life, who missed his friends and the familiarity of Utah, immediately asked, his voice tight, "Can I go back to Utah? Like, now?" Owen, overhearing, asked if he could go too. Before noon that same Friday, I had two of my boys on an airplane back to Utah, heading towards the relative stability of my family there.

William, ever my protector, initially decided he wanted to stay with me, his face set with a fierce loyalty, feeling he couldn't leave me alone to face this. However, knowing how uncomfortable the atmosphere in the house would be at a minimum, and genuinely unsure of how Keith might act after the confrontation and in the days that followed, I encouraged all the boys to go to Utah where they would be safer and more insulated from the immediate fallout.

The weight of the situation, perhaps the desire to be with his brothers, and my encouragement, led William to ask to return to Utah the next day. He was on a plane shortly after, leaving me truly alone in the house that was no longer a home. The speed of it all felt surreal, like an out-of-body experience.

While a part of me, the part that still clung to disbelief, didn't want to see the proof, didn't want to read the words that would make it undeniably real, I knew I needed to. Owen had seen the messages while using our VR headset, which was logged into Keith's Facebook account. Private messages had been popping up on the screen— messages between Keith and his mistress, a woman he had met at work.

It appeared, from the snippets Owen had glimpsed before quickly closing it down, horrified, that they had been having an emotional affair for several months already, filled with declarations of love and plans for a future. I had the messages queued up, ready to display on the large TV screen in our living room, a weapon held in reserve if I needed them when Keith came home for lunch. My heart hammered against my ribs, a sick, heavy beat.

As soon as he walked in the door for lunch, his tone was cold, his demeanor sluggish, almost like he knew what was about to happen. He could tell something was profoundly wrong. The air in the house was thick with unspoken accusations, with my barely contained grief and rage. I saw it in his eyes as they met mine, the way his usual smile was absent, I heard it in the cautious, almost fearful tone of his voice as he asked, "What's going on, babe?"

I looked him straight in the eye, my own gaze unwavering, cold. "Do you have something to tell me, Keith?"

At first, he denied it. He feigned ignorance, and tried to deflect with questions about my day. Even when I mentioned her name, the name Owen had seen, the name that was now seared into my brain, he tried to play dumb, his voice attempting a lightness that didn't reach his eyes. "What? My colleague? What about her?"

"Keith," I said, my voice dangerously calm, each word precise, "I'm not dumb."

And finally, faced with my cold certainty, the dam broke. He admitted it. The carefully constructed facade crumbled, revealing the deceit beneath. He admitted to having an affair.

When I asked him why—why he would do this after everything we'd built, after the vows, after the life I thought we shared, after everything I thought he felt for me—his answer blindsided me, a fresh wave of betrayal washing over the first. He said it was because of the problems we had been having in our marriage.

Problems? That caught me completely off guard. He claimed these "problems," these supposed issues I was apparently unaware of, were leading him to want to leave me. He told me, his voice flat, devoid of the emotion I was drowning in, that he'd fallen out of love two years prior. Two years. Before we even moved to Texas.

He claimed the move itself, the beautiful house, the pool, the "fresh start" we were supposed to be having, was his last-ditch effort, a secret, unspoken hope to save our marriage—a hope, a plan, a dissatisfaction he had never once conveyed to me.

I was completely, utterly in the dark. Yes, we had disagreements, arguments like any couple over seven years. But I didn't feel like we'd ever had a fight we hadn't resolved, a wound that hadn't been tended to. Anytime I had sensed a shift in him, felt a subtle distance growing between us, a coolness in his demeanor, I had asked him directly, "Is something wrong? Are you unhappy? Are we okay?"

And every single time, he had looked me in the eye and reassured me, told me no, everything was fine, that he loved me. Lies. All lies.

Blindsided. Devastated. Heartbroken. The man I loved, the man I thought loved me in return, the man I believed was my "W," my wholeness, my safe harbor, had been living a lie for years. The safe haven I thought we'd built together, brick by brick, was a facade, a carefully constructed illusion.

But even through the shock, the disbelief, the shattering pain that threatened to consume me, a familiar, steely resolve, born of countless past betrayals, rose within me. I deserved better than this. I knew, in that moment, with absolute, soul-deep certainty, that I was done.

There was no going back, no fixing this betrayal. I had a suitcase already packed for him. I pointed to it and told him I was filing for divorce.

This life I had painstakingly built, the stability I had craved and fought for, the man I loved—everything felt tainted, questioned. Every moment, every shared memory over the past seven years suddenly felt suspect, cast in the harsh, unflattering light of his deceit. Was any of it real? Had he cheated before? I couldn't discern truth from fiction anymore.

My reality felt fractured, my heart absolutely broken, shattered into a million pieces. The light I thought I'd seen at the end of the tunnel after Saprea had been extinguished, plunging me back into darkness, into another agonizing chapter of loss and betrayal.

CHAPTER 35

(E)cho

Rocked by the realization of what had happened, stunned by the abrupt and devastating end of my marriage to Keith, I retreated into the immediate aftermath.

There was a moment that day—after the confrontation, after the boys were on a plane to Utah, after the initial adrenaline surge of action mode subsided—when the full weight of the betrayal crashed down. I remember standing in my bathroom, leaning against the cool tiles of the shower wall, the scent of Keith's now-absent shampoo still faintly lingering in the air. The sobs started as a tremor deep in my chest and then ripped through me, violent and wracking.

I was bawling my eyes out, gasping for breath, feeling the type of raw, eviscerating pain I hadn't felt before. Because I had never been in love the way that I loved Keith. So securely. So safely. So real. Or so I had believed with every fiber of my being. This wasn't just disappointment; this felt like a part of my soul being torn away.

Yet, amidst the gut-wrenching sobs, as I slid down the wall to the cold floor, a strange, almost detached thought surfaced—a flicker of relief. As the tears flowed, I realized, with a startling, unwelcome clarity, that he was no longer my responsibility. It was a chilling echo of how I'd felt after leaving Eric, but magnified.

My relationship with Keith had been vastly different from my relationship with Eric. I truly felt I was in love with Keith—deeply and wholly—in a way that had felt transformative. But in hindsight, even in those early moments of acute heartbreak, sitting on the bathroom floor, the pattern started to emerge with sickening clarity.

I had married two very similar men. Men who carried their own unresolved trauma, their own deep-seated insecurities that they didn't know how to deal with constructively. Men who, when faced with their own shortcomings or unhappiness, seemed more comfortable residing in the victim role, blaming external circumstances or others rather than truly feeling their feelings, taking responsibility, and working through their pain.

Over the course of our seven-year relationship, Keith had cycled through more than a dozen different jobs. Each one started with enthusiasm—a new hope—only to dissolve into complaints, dissatisfaction, and an eventual departure. More than two years of our time together had been marked by his unemployment, the financial strain adding another layer of stress to our lives.

When we first met, he was making more money than me—a fact that perhaps subtly played into traditional provider roles. But as soon as I transitioned into the tech industry, my earnings quickly surpassed his, and continued to grow at a rapid rate. This financial disparity, I slowly realized, was something that was always difficult for him—a constant, unspoken source of underlying tension.

Anytime something good happened for me professionally—a promotion, a successful project, positive recognition from my peers or managers—I knew that inevitably, while he would offer a smile and congratulations, it would often be followed by a comment tinged with his own dissatisfaction: "That's great, babe. I wonder when something like that is going to happen for me." Or, "You're so lucky; things just seem to fall into place for you."

His inability to genuinely celebrate my successes without immediately comparing them to his own perceived lack thereof—without that subtle undercurrent of resentment or envy—eroded our connection. I became hesitant to even share my achievements.

I realized, with a sinking feeling of self-reproach, that I had repeated a damaging pattern. I did with Keith what I had done with Eric: at first, I tried to fix him. I tried to fix everything for him—spending hours researching different jobs that might suit him, polishing his résumé, encouraging him to move from one position to another when, inevitably, after just a month or two into a new role, he would start expressing how miserable he was.

Every day after work felt like *Groundhog Day,* listening to his litany of unhappiness, the unfairness of his boss, the tedium of his tasks. I'd try to offer solutions, to brainstorm, to manage his emotions alongside my own and those of my children, exhausting myself in the process.

The difference—the reason this betrayal cut so much deeper than the end of my first marriage—was that Keith and I were friends. Or so I believed. We genuinely had fun together, especially in the beginning. We enjoyed watching and talking sports, going camping and four-wheeling, and taking spontaneous road trips.

We shared similar interests and spent a significant amount of our time together. Looking back now, I see that intense togetherness—his apparent lack of outside friendships, his disinterest in forming any—not as a sign of deep devotion, but as a potential red flag. A sign of codependency, perhaps. An unhealthy enmeshment that left little room for individual growth or outside support systems.

So, in that moment of relief mixed with immense sadness, standing amidst the emotional wreckage of my second marriage, I also knew—with a certainty born of too much past experience—that I was going to be able to move forward. This time was different in crucial ways.

This time, I was financially stable, thanks to the career I had fought so hard to build. This time, I had my boys. And while their hearts were hurting too—confused and betrayed by another father figure—I wasn't facing the added trauma of a bitter custody battle.

I got the house listed for sale within weeks. The process of staging, showing, and eventually selling the beautiful home we had built together in Texas felt like another layer of grief, dismantling the physical manifestation of our shared life. Preparing the house, packing boxes filled with seven years of memories, organizing the logistics of yet another major life upheaval—it all kept me relentlessly busy, providing a necessary, if temporary, distraction from the gaping wound in my heart.

But I also did something familiar. Something I always did in times of acute emotional distress—a pattern I was only just beginning to recognize as unhealthy. I immediately returned to online dating.

Seeking attention. Validation. A temporary balm for the pain. A way to prove to myself I was still desirable after such a profound rejection. I was naïve—perhaps willfully so—thinking that this time would be different.

That the lessons I thought I had learned since my first divorce, the healing I thought I'd achieved at Saprea, would protect me. I believed I could navigate the dating world with more wisdom. Stronger boundaries.

What I failed to fully realize then—in the rawness of that fresh betrayal—was how much of my trauma, my learned behaviors, my coping mechanisms, and even the lingering indoctrination from my upbringing were still deeply embedded within me. They were like dormant seeds, waiting for the right conditions—stress, loneliness, a perceived rejection—to be triggered.

Ready to pull me back into familiar, unhealthy patterns despite the progress I thought I'd made.

The journey towards true, sustainable wholeness was far from over.

CHAPTER 36

(R)eturn

The silence in the house felt deafening, amplifying my aloneness. My phone buzzing with notifications, new matches, messages, attention from men who, just weeks earlier, I might never have crossed paths with, a welcome break to the silence. The sheer volume was overwhelming, feeding that old, familiar need for external validation, but also making it harder to discern genuine connection from fleeting interest or potential danger.

Each "like" or message was a tiny dopamine hit, a temporary distraction from the gaping wound Keith had left.

I remember one gentleman I connected with early on. Upon finding out how recently my marriage had ended—literally just days before—he offered some unsolicited but, in hindsight, incredibly wise advice during one of our first chats. He told me bluntly, though not unkindly, that I wasn't ready for anything remotely serious, that

I needed to take significant time for myself to heal before even thinking about jumping back into dating.

I remember scoffing internally at his words, a wave of defensiveness washing over me. *Who does he think he is? He doesn't know me.* I wanted to believe I was ready, that I could handle it, that this time would be different. That I wouldn't repeat past mistakes.

But now, looking back with the clarity of hindsight and more healing, I know just how right he was. I wasn't ready. I was using dating as a crutch, a potent distraction, a way to avoid the immense pain of betrayal and the daunting, terrifying task of sitting with my grief and healing the wounds that made me so vulnerable in the first place.

Despite that sound advice, and against my better judgment, I met someone relatively quickly who I ended up spending several weeks with. In that raw, immediate aftermath of Keith's departure, the companionship provided exactly what I craved: distraction from the empty house, constant attention that filled the silence, a semblance of care, and the feeling of being wanted by someone new.

I genuinely enjoyed my time with him; it felt good to be seen and desired after the shock of the betrayal—to laugh again, to feel, however superficially, connected. But my deep-seated insecurities, never far beneath the surface, soon reared their ugly heads. The fear of abandonment, the desperate need for constant reassurance—it all surfaced with an intensity that surprised even me.

I quickly ruined that budding relationship by trying to push things towards exclusivity far too quickly, needing labels and commitments to quiet my anxiety. Ultimately, I suffocated something that might have been a harmless distraction before it had a chance to breathe. *Another one bites the dust,* I thought, the familiar shame settling in.

During this turbulent time, while still living in Texas and frantically getting the house ready to sell—sorting through seven years of accumulated belongings, each item a potential landmine of memory—I traveled back to Utah on a couple of different occasions. One of those trips was for Christmas, and it would culminate in one of the worst, most public anxiety attacks I have ever experienced.

My sister's house, usually a place of comfort, was full of extended family and friends—primarily from my dad's side. These were people I was slowly, painfully realizing I needed to heal from, not with, because there seemed to be no collective desire among many of them to acknowledge or address the wounds of the past.

Being surrounded by them, by their festive cheer, their laughter, their seemingly uncomplicated lives, while I was drowning internally in the fresh grief of my marriage ending and the old grief tied to family dynamics, felt unbearable. The house, filled with the scent of pine needles, baking cookies, and too many people, felt claustrophobic.

Every polite inquiry about how I was doing felt like a potential trigger. Every cheerful Christmas carol felt like a mockery of my internal pain.

Overwhelmed, feeling the walls closing in, I escaped downstairs to what I hoped would be the quiet of the basement. But the tears started—hot and unstoppable—quickly escalating into uncontrollable, gasping sobs and then terrifying hyperventilation. My chest felt like it was in a vise.

My sister, mom, and boys, hearing my distress, came rushing down, their faces etched with concern. They tried to help, to soothe me. My mom, whose soft touch and calm voice could normally help me breathe through an anxiety attack, couldn't get me to calm down this time.

The panic was too immense, too consuming, fueled by layers of fresh and old pain. My sister, seeing my escalating distress and the way I was struggling to breathe, ended up calling 911. The arrival of paramedics, the questions, the oxygen mask—it was all a blur of humiliation and terror.

That moment—needing emergency intervention simply to cope with the emotional pain of being in that specific family environment—was a terrifying wake-up call. I knew then that the pain I was feeling, this new grief of losing the future I thought I had with Keith, layered onto the old family trauma, was so deep and intense that healing would take much longer—and likely require more intensive help—than I had hoped or thought.

I returned to Texas after the holidays, the memory of the Christmas breakdown still vivid, still shameful. I continued navigating the dating scene, desperate to fill the void, while our house was being shown to potential buyers. Remarkably, the house sold quickly—a small mercy in the chaos.

Within three months of learning about Keith's affair, I had sold the house, packed up our remaining belongings into a U-Haul, and was driving back to Utah, the Texas landscape receding in my rearview mirror. In some ways, I was almost more upset about having to return to Utah than about the marriage ending.

Utah—the place I had finally escaped, the place I had sworn I would never live in again. Utah—the geographical container for so much of my past trauma, a place I was scared to return to, especially in such a state of despair, defeat, and vulnerability.

Upon arriving back, the mountains that once felt like home now loomed over me with a sense of judgment. The first six months were utterly miserable. I was depressed, angry, grieving the loss of my marriage, the loss of my Texas life, the loss of the future I had envisioned.

Added to my own pain was the palpable pain of my three boys, who were also dealing with their own anger, confusion, and sadness at losing a stepdad they had once truly loved and admired. Scott's recent diagnosis of bipolar disorder, coupled with the upheaval of another divorce in their young lives, made finding stability and professional support paramount.

I knew I needed to find a good therapist for all of them—someone equipped to handle their complex needs, someone who could help them navigate this new reality. I focused my search on finding a therapist who was not LDS, believing a secular perspective would be more beneficial. I also hoped for a male therapist, understanding the dire need for my boys to have a positive male influence in their life. And I wanted someone who approached things from a more holistic, person-centered viewpoint rather than a rigid, purely textbook approach.

After many calls and inquiries, I found someone who seemed to fit the bill. He was, from the outset, wonderful with my boys, creating a safe space for them to express their difficult emotions.

His impact extended beyond my children during a moment of profound crisis. At one point, Scott got very sick again due to complications from his diabetes and bladder disorder and was admitted to the ICU. He was despondent, physically and emotionally depleted, ready to give up.

Out of sheer desperation, feeling utterly helpless, watching my child suffer, I texted his therapist, begging for help, for guidance, for anything. He responded immediately and, to my astonishment, came to the hospital.

He sat with me in the sterile, beeping environment of the ICU waiting room for thirty minutes, simply listening with profound empathy as I poured out my pain, my fear, my despair at not knowing how to help my son. In that moment of compassionate presence—of being truly heard without judgment—I realized he could potentially be a good therapist for me, too.

The therapist I had seen for years had been amazing, providing crucial healing at a time I needed it, but I felt strongly that a male perspective, particularly from someone who had shown such genuine empathy and understanding in a moment of crisis, could be beneficial now.

I started seeing him myself. Within the first couple of months, he said something that would, unexpectedly, change the course of my life again. He listened to my grief, my anger, my resentment towards Utah and the circumstances that had forced my return. Then, he gently but firmly told me that wallowing in my anger towards Utah wasn't helping.

He told me I needed to get out into my community. At first, I was angry at his suggestion. I just wanted him to hear and validate my pain, my bitterness towards the place that held so many bad memories.

But he didn't let me stay there. Instead, he insisted that I was going to get out into the community—that I was going to find healing in the community—in the very place where so much of my trauma had happened. He believed I needed to reclaim my power within that environment, to rewrite my relationship with the place itself.

He happened to be planning a small, intimate wine-tasting event shortly after this conversation and invited me to come. My immediate reaction was discomfort, intense resistance. I imagined a room full of sophisticated, beautiful people, wealthy, dressed impeccably—a world where I felt I didn't belong, where I would feel judged, out of place, inadequate.

The old insecurities flared. But he encouraged me gently, persistently. Reluctantly, terrified but also a little intrigued, I accepted the invite.

That night, attending that wine event—forcing myself to walk into that room—changed so much for me. The space was filled with art, music, and yes, people who seemed confident and put-together. It was the first time in a long time I allowed myself to be part of a group of mostly strangers, pushing past my intense discomfort and social anxiety for the sake and the hope of growth.

And growth did happen. It wasn't instantaneous, but stepping into that uncomfortable space, challenging my assumptions and fears, planted a seed. It was the tentative beginning of re-engaging with the world around me in a new way—not about seeking romantic validation, but about finding connection and community.

It would still take time, more work, more healing, but it felt like another crucial step forward on the long, winding journey.

CHAPTER 37

(U)tah

———◆———

Before I ever set foot back in Utah, before the mountains loomed over me with their familiar mix of beauty and judgment, there was the long drive home from Texas.

The flat, open plains slowly gave way to the towering Wasatch Front as I listened to *Codependent No More* by Melody Beattie. Each word, each example, felt like both an indictment and a revelation. The narrator's calm voice filled the car, explaining patterns of behavior that were eerily, uncomfortably familiar.

It was the first time I truly understood the insidious nature of codependency. I saw myself in nearly every page—this compulsive need to fix others, to save them, to derive my worth from their perceived need for me. I realized it stemmed from the deep, unhealed trauma of not believing I could fix myself, of secretly wanting someone else to save me.

If I could give that feeling to someone else—if I could make them feel seen, safe, even temporarily healed—why wouldn't I? It felt noble. Purposeful. But coupled with being raised in a high-demand religion that often framed a woman's worth through selfless service, it made painful sense why I had spent both my marriages, and so many relationships in between, caring for everyone else while neglecting myself.

Having the language for these patterns felt like a first, crucial step toward change.

In the solitude of that drive, I made a plan: I would avoid the Utah dating scene altogether. My heart still yearned for the anonymity and fresh start Texas had briefly offered. My revised goal was to eventually find someone I could have a long-distance relationship with—someone to talk to, care about, and receive validation from, but who wouldn't consume my daily life. That way, my time and energy in Utah could go toward my boys, helping them settle after another upheaval.

It was a good plan. But it didn't last long.

Once the chaos of moving subsided, the loneliness set in like an ache. Despite my best intentions, I found myself back on the dating apps—the familiar glow of my phone screen a comforting, if ultimately hollow, companion. I told myself this time was different. That I was more selective. That I was dating from a place of awareness rather than crisis.

But looking back, I can see how quickly I slipped into the same patterns—drawn to familiar dynamics, still subconsciously hoping to heal old wounds through new, unsuitable partners.

Each dating experience, however brief, came with its own lesson. There were the men whose intentions were obvious almost immediately—the blatant objectification, the rush toward sex, the disrespect. I learned to end those quickly. Then there were the more skillful ones: charming, attentive, saying all the right things. They could hold my attention for weeks, sometimes months, until their own unhealed wounds surfaced and the connection unraveled.

One of my most persistent trauma responses is seeking closure where none exists—revisiting bad situations, hoping for a different ending, punishing myself by staying connected to men who cannot give me what I need. It's a compulsion to prove my worth to those unwilling or unable to value me.

I also met genuinely good, decent men—kind, respectful, emotionally stable. And yet, when something real began to form, my anxious attachment flared. Fear of losing myself. Fear of heartbreak. I'd sabotage the connection before it could deepen. On the flip side, if someone came on too strong, love-bombing with gifts and attention, I'd be both drawn in and deeply suspicious.

Dating became its own messy, painful form of self-discovery. The men who were willing to be honest with me—to point out my patterns with compassion—were invaluable. Their words forced me to look at myself in ways I hadn't before.

The truth was, I didn't know how to be alone. The silence was unbearable, especially after Keith's betrayal. I tried to posture as the victor, not the victim—rising above, moving forward. But in doing so, I robbed myself of the chance to fully grieve.

Predictably, I engaged in behaviors that put me at risk—not as extreme as after my first divorce, but still careless. Meeting strangers too quickly. Ignoring red flags because I was lonely. Oversharing with men I barely knew. Only in hindsight, after talking it through with my therapist or friends, did I realize how easily things could have gone wrong.

It was during this time that I met someone who was open about living with PTSD and being in therapy. I told myself this was different—that I wasn't trying to fix him, that my role was simply to offer patience and understanding because of my own knowledge around trauma. I thought it was empathy, not codependency.

But almost immediately, red flags appeared. I brushed them aside, telling myself he was still working through things—just as I was—when, in truth, I was willfully ignoring patterns that made me uneasy. I was still prioritizing someone else's healing over my own, still pouring energy into someone who wasn't truly doing the work.

That realization was sobering. Patience is only healthy when it's mutual, when the other person is equally invested in growth. Otherwise, it's just another form of self-abandonment.

Around the same time, I was talking to my son, Scott, about responsibility and patterns. Suddenly, another piece of my codependency clicked into place: I have never not been taking care of someone. The oldest of five, always helping with kids in our home. Babysitting as soon as I could. Moving away at twenty to be a nanny. Meeting Eric, having three children. Then marrying Keith and taking on his responsibilities.

I have spent my entire adult life in a caretaking role, often to the detriment of my own needs. Abuse taught me my needs didn't matter. Religion reinforced that service and sacrifice defined my worth.

Together, they created a perfect storm for my need to fix and save others—often at my own expense.

With this awareness, I knew I had to make real changes. I needed to learn how to exist without rescuing someone else—and without needing to be rescued myself.

That shift wasn't going to happen overnight. It would require boundaries I'd never truly enforced before, a level of self-prioritization I wasn't used to, and a commitment to stop pouring my energy into people who weren't willing to match it. But for the first time, I could see the pattern clearly. And once I saw it, I couldn't unsee it.

CHAPTER 38

(S)hift

At this point, nearly two years had passed since my divorce from Keith. The raw, immediate pain had dulled somewhat, replaced by a weary understanding of my own patterns. The realization that I needed to make major, fundamental changes was clearer than ever, but actually implementing those changes—rewiring decades of learned behavior and trauma responses—remained incredibly difficult. I knew it would take time, immense patience with myself, and deliberate, conscious baby steps.

One piece of advice echoed repeatedly from therapists, self-help books, and well-meaning friends whenever I found myself single again: *Be single. Be alone. Learn how to be alone.* Logically, I understood it. But emotionally, it was advice I always resisted, always feared. The thought of true solitude, of not having the distraction or validation of a romantic pursuit, felt terrifying. My internal landscape could be a scary place, and being alone meant confronting it without a buffer.

I didn't want to get to a place where I was so okay with being alone, so self-sufficient, that I closed myself off entirely to the possibility of a healthy, loving partnership. Despite all the heartbreak and betrayals, a resilient part of me still truly believed that with the healing I had done, the career I had built, the self-forgiveness and self-love I was painstakingly cultivating, the next time I fell in love, it could be unlike anything I had ever experienced. I wanted that potential; I didn't want to take that opportunity away from myself by shutting down completely.

So, while I knew I still had a lot of healing to do, taking dating entirely off the table felt like admitting defeat—like giving up on a core human desire for connection.

But at the beginning of 2025, after a particularly painful and disillusioning dating experience, something shifted. I made a vow to myself, a serious, committed vow: I would get off all the dating apps. No more swiping, no more superficial connections, no more chasing dopamine hits from new matches.

This single action removed the vast majority of my previous dating opportunities, as apps had become my primary, almost exclusive, way of meeting men. I hadn't promised myself I wouldn't date if an organic connection happened—just that I wouldn't actively pursue it through the apps, or make it the focus of my energy or my evenings.

One of the reasons staying off the apps had always been so difficult was my intense FOMO—fear of missing out. I was always worried about missing *the one* if I wasn't constantly swiping, constantly available, constantly searching. *What if he's out there looking for me right now on this app?* was a powerful lure.

However, something else had been happening concurrently over the last two years—a slower, more organic shift, largely at the gentle but persistent direction of my therapist. I had gotten out into my community.

What started tentatively with that first awkward but ultimately empowering wine event my therapist encouraged me to attend had snowballed into a social life I never saw coming—one built on shared interests and genuine connection rather than romantic pursuit. I was immersing myself in different groups, connecting with diverse types of people.

I networked through tech events related to my career, finding common ground with colleagues outside of work. I became involved in different charitable events, finding a quiet purpose in giving back, in contributing to something larger than myself. I attended events focused on female empowerment, workshops on healing and growth, connecting with strong, inspiring women whose stories resonated with my own.

Every time I went to any type of event—birthday parties, a community fundraiser, a professional development seminar—I inevitably met somebody new I connected with on some level, often unexpectedly.

A surprising and deeply affirming pattern began to emerge: an almost palpable energy where survivors seemed to see and feel each other, drawn together almost magnetically. It didn't matter the type of event; I was frequently meeting other women who had also been abused, who were on their own healing journeys, who understood the unspoken language of trauma and resilience.

Sharing stories in these safe spaces, offering mutual support, feeling truly understood without having to over-explain—it was incredibly powerful, a balm to old wounds.

It was through one of these new community connections that I met Jess. She sold Mary Kay, and her energy was magnetic—bright, fun, and grounded all at once. After a few conversations, she asked if I would be interested in joining her team.

My initial reaction was skepticism; I had done direct sales before, and it wasn't something I cared to do again. But Jess didn't lead with sales talk. She talked about the sisterhood, the community of women who celebrated one another's wins, and the personal growth that came with being part of it. That part made me pause.

I told her I was only joining for that sense of community and connection—not to expect big sales from me. But the more I got involved—attending meetings, trying the products—the more I found myself genuinely loving them. I started using the products daily, not for anyone else, but because it made me feel good. More than that, the friendships I built there became invaluable.

Somewhere along the way, Mary Kay stopped being just a fun extra thing I was doing with Jess's team—it became another piece of my healing. And it felt oddly full-circle, because the very first time I was ever introduced to Mary Kay was at my grandma's house.

I can still picture it—pink compacts on her bathroom counter, the smell of powder, the glossy lipsticks lined up like little soldiers. Back then, I thought Mary Kay was for "fancy" women, the kind who wore perfume to the grocery store and always had their hair curled just so.

I never imagined that decades later, I'd find myself in my own bathroom, opening the same pink compacts, not because I was trying to look like someone else, but because I had finally become a woman I admired—confident, grounded, and unapologetically myself.

* * *

As I continued to immerse myself in this burgeoning social life, I was slowly, almost without realizing it at first, building a community I had needed for so long—one entirely outside of my family and outside of the often-judgmental LDS church culture that had been the only culture I had really known in Utah. Suddenly, I was finding genuine love and acceptance here, within a community I hadn't known existed before, one built on shared values, mutual respect, and authentic connection.

And somewhere in the middle of that new life, I met someone.

When we first crossed paths, I didn't feel the intense, all-consuming pull I used to mistake for love. There were no butterflies, no urgent need to define what we were. It was calm. Easy. Months could pass between seeing each other, and it didn't shake anything.

I kept seeing other people—not because I didn't care, but because I knew he didn't want anything serious. At the time, I didn't yet know how to hold space for something gentle. I was still unlearning the idea that love had to be urgent to be real.

What I didn't realize then was that real love sometimes builds quietly, without announcements or deadlines. While I was out looking for chemistry and clarity, something safer and more sustainable was taking root.

He was consistent. Respectful. Steady. And for the first time in my life, I didn't try to force it into shape. I just let it be.

Looking back now, I'm grateful for that. If I'd recognized its depth too soon, I might have clung to it, tried to define it, or pushed it into something it wasn't ready to be. Instead, it unfolded naturally, at its own pace.

Today, I get to experience a connection that feels grounded, secure, and real. Time together is spent in peace, laughter, and ease. There's no pressure to perform, no constant fear of the other shoe dropping. His actions speak louder than words, and I've learned to trust what they say.

The calm I feel with him is unlike anything I've known before. I'm not clinging or bracing for loss. I'm simply present.

Whatever this becomes—whether it lasts a lifetime or just a season—I know I'll be grateful for it. Grateful for the reminder that love can meet you where you are instead of demanding you twist yourself into someone else's shape.

Because here's the truth: I healed me. He didn't save me. But in his presence, I've been able to see the version of myself I fought so hard to become—a woman who loves from a place of wholeness, not need.

For the first time in my life, I'm falling in love with someone who loves the me who is already in love with herself. And that changes everything.

CHAPTER 39

(W)hole

The journey from the bottom of that hole described in the prologue – the despair of arrest, the cold steel of handcuffs, the crushing weight of past mistakes, the feeling of being utterly broken and silenced – has been long, arduous, and anything but linear. It has been a slow, often painful, climb towards the light, towards understanding, towards healing. And one of the most challenging, yet ultimately most empowering, aspects of that ascent has been rediscovering and learning to wield my own voice.

For so long, it felt like a fragile thing, easily crushed, easily dismissed. During the period of abuse by my grandfather, I vividly recall the few instances I dared to express discomfort or pain, only to be met with his chilling, dismissive stare, or worse, the quiet threat, "If you tell anyone, YOU will be in big trouble," his musk cologne a suffocating blanket. To speak up and be silenced, to have your reality denied by the very person causing the harm, adds another layer of profound violation to the already immense burden. It instills a deep-seated hesitation, a fear that lodges in your throat, a reluctance to ever speak your truth again for fear of invalidation or retribution.

When I did find the courage to speak up, to tell my parents about my grandfather, that initial act of using my voice was met with their pained doubt, their desperate questions about the possibility of my mistaking a harmless touch for what I had described.

Even after my grandfather admitted his actions and the authorities became involved, using my voice often felt more detrimental than empowering. The disclosure ripped through our family, turning my world upside down. Instead of feeling protected or vindicated, I constantly felt like I was the one in trouble, the one causing the disruption, the one whose words had unleashed chaos.

As I matured, or rather, as I stumbled through adolescence, my once timid and respectful voice, conditioned by fear and religious expectation, morphed into a loud, angry, and often defiant one. It was a raw, unprocessed reaction to years of feeling unheard, unseen, and controlled. The tighter my parents tried to control my life and the choices I made – choices often fueled by the very trauma they seemed unable or unwilling to fully address – the more I rebelled, my voice becoming a weapon of defiance rather than a tool for connection.

Therapy sessions during those years, often mandated, proved ineffective in providing the support or tools I needed to navigate the complex emotions of anger, grief, and betrayal. My parents' frustration with my behavior only grew, creating a chasm between us.

Church, once a place I associated with community and belonging, suddenly felt like a source of judgment and profound disappointment, where lessons on forgiveness felt like personal accusations against my inability to simply "get over" the profound injustice that had shaped my young life.

My anger and frustration, having no healthy outlet, manifested in destructive ways. There were explosive outbursts directed at my parents and siblings, words hurled like stones. However, the harshest, most relentless anger was reserved for myself. I internalized the pain, the blame, the pervasive feeling of being inherently "bad," damaged goods. This led to years of self-deprecating thoughts, a constant internal chorus of negativity, and at times, even self-harm – scratching at my arms and face until they were raw and marked during moments of intense emotional distress, a physical manifestation of the invisible wounds.

The emotional turmoil I was experiencing had taken a devastating toll on my self-image, leading to a cascade of destructive behaviors and a deepening sense of self-loathing. I felt trapped in a seemingly endless cycle of pain and anger, unable to find a way out, my true voice lost somewhere in the wreckage.

During my adolescence, whenever I did attempt to express my thoughts or feelings, especially if they contradicted my parents' views or rules, I was often met with accusations of being disrespectful, of "talking back," and subsequently punished with grounding.

The constant reprimands and punishments only served to widen the gap between my parents and me, hindering any possibility of open and honest communication and reinforcing my deeply ingrained belief that my voice didn't matter, or worse, that it was inherently wrong.

The aftermath of the fake robbery when I was eighteen provided another harsh lesson in the potential consequences of using my voice, even when attempting to rectify a wrong. When my conscience finally won out and I decided to use my voice to assist the police in solving the string of other robberies Chad had committed, hoping perhaps for some redemption or gratitude, I was met instead with broken promises from detectives and, ultimately, a jail cell. The betrayal stung deeply.

Then came the arson attack on my car, which felt like a direct, violent consequence of speaking out against Chad and his associates, driving home the terrifying reality that using my voice could bring tangible danger, reinforcing the insidious idea that silence might indeed be safer.

Even in moments that should have been entirely my own, moments of personal choice and agency, my voice often faltered. When Eric proposed at the cabin, amidst the whirlwind of emotions surrounding my unexpected pregnancy, I lacked the assertiveness, the self-trust, to decline, to express my deep reservations or fears.

When we exchanged vows, my true feelings, my anxieties about the future, were drowned out by a chorus of external pressures – the expectations of my parents, the teachings of my church about the sanctity of marriage and family, and even my own internalized beliefs about what I should want, what a "good" woman would do. I felt trapped in a role I wasn't ready for, my own desires and dreams overshadowed by the immense weight of societal and familial expectations, my inner voice silenced by obligation.

My attempts to communicate with my grandfather's second wife about his past—and the impact of his actions—were met with swift and painful dismissal. In 2016, during a desperate time when I was terrified that Eric might try to move the boys away from me, I reached out to her via Facebook Messenger, pleading for financial help to hire a lawyer. Her response was laced with deflection and a passive-aggressive undertone. She wrote, "I don't know what exactly went on between you and your grandfather," a statement that implied I had been a willing participant—that it was some kind of mutual entanglement rather than abuse. Her feigned ignorance wasn't just hurtful; it was cruel. Another dig disguised as confusion. Another way of saying: I don't want to know.

Later, when I confided in my own grandmother that I had reached out to my grandfather's widow for help, her response wasn't empathy for my desperate situation, but disappointment in me for having contacted her at all. It was another painful reinforcement of the message that my voice, my needs, my pain stemming from the abuse, were inconvenient, unwelcome, perhaps even shameful to the family system.

This theme of having to defend myself, of being belittled or disbelieved, even bled into my interactions with religious authority figures.

After my father reported my relationship with Mitch, the married man, I was disfellowshipped. During that initial bishop's council, I confessed every sin I could recall, accepting my punishment with the explicit promise that I would never have to repeat those painful details again, that a transcript would suffice if leadership changed. Yet, years later, seeking reinstatement in Philadelphia, a new bishopric, strangers to me, made me recount everything, only to deny my request, deeming me "not yet worthy." It was another institutional betrayal, another promise broken, another instance where my vulnerable truth was met not with grace, but with judgment.

Throughout my career, paradoxically, I often did find and use my voice to address wrongdoing, to stand up for myself or others, sometimes resulting in termination from employers who preferred compliance over critical feedback. I also faced targeted attacks from colleagues threatened by my willingness to hold them accountable. It seemed using my voice professionally had consequences, just as it often did personally. It felt like a constant battle, stepping up to the plate time and time again, only to strike out, to be misunderstood, dismissed, or punished.

With a batting average that felt like .000, giving up would have been the logical, perhaps even sensible, thing to do. But quitting, truly surrendering my right to speak, is simply not in my nature.

That stubborn streak my mother recognized in me as a toddler, the one she chose to nurture rather than extinguish, perhaps became my saving grace. Despite the repeated failures, the constant sense of disappointment, the fear of repercussions, I refused to throw in the towel. I was determined, somewhere deep inside, to find a way to overcome these challenges, to make my voice heard effectively, and perhaps, finally, to have it lead not to further pain, but to justice, to healing, to connection.

Discovering the concept of tonic immobility, understanding that my body's freeze response was a natural, involuntary survival mechanism, not a failure on my part, was profoundly validating. Reading books like *The Body Keeps the Score* and *No Bad Parts*, understanding the science behind trauma's impact on the brain and body, allowed me to finally separate my actions from my inherent worth, paving the way for true self-forgiveness. Engaging with Internal Family Systems, learning to speak to and validate the wounded parts of my younger self with compassion, added another crucial layer of healing, teaching me to listen to and trust my own internal voice.

In 2017, years after the assault by Andrew, a phone call from my sister about a lawyer who specialized in civil cases for sexual assault changed everything. I filed a lawsuit to confront him legally—a profound act of reclaiming my voice and taking back power within the very system that had once failed me so miserably. After nearly a year of trying to serve him, the judge finally granted me a court date. Andrew was a no-show—his voice, once so loud and threatening, suddenly silent. Still, I was sworn in. And for the first time, I was listened to, believed, and handed a small sliver of justice: the judge ruled in my favor.

But, even seeking justice or compensation for unrelated events, like a car accident that left me with post-concussive syndrome, often forced me back into the agonizing position of defending my past trauma.

During mediation with the insurance company, their lawyer, in a clear attempt to discredit me, asked if I'd ever sued anyone else. When I truthfully answered yes, referring to the civil suit against Andrew, she pressed for details, forcing me to recount the rape in that sterile, adversarial environment. It was a profound invasion, my deepest wounds weaponized to suggest I was merely litigious. I stood firm, looked her in the eye, and told the truth, refusing to be broken or shamed by her tactics, but the experience was another stark reminder of how my past could be used to silence or invalidate my present voice.

The civil court victory against Andrew was monumental in its emotional impact. It wasn't about the money; it was about a judge listening—acknowledging my suffering, validating my testimony. For the first time, in relation to my deepest traumas, I felt truly heard and believed by an impartial authority figure. That experience, combined with the empowerment I found in sharing my story publicly at work, the incredible support from the people at Saprea and the women who had become sisters, and the connections forged within the online survivor community, solidified the undeniable power of speaking truth—of owning one's narrative.

Through all these experiences, one of the most valuable lessons I've learned is mastering the art of effective communication—understanding when and how to express myself, and modulating emotion to fit the situation. Sometimes passion and raw honesty are crucial; other times, a more neutral, objective tone is what allows me to be truly heard. Learning to control my reactions, to choose my battles, to speak from a place of grounded strength rather than reactive anger, has been key.

One of the most profound "everything happens for a reason" moments came years later, when my own son bravely told me that someone who was supposed to protect him had crossed a line—laying hands on him in anger. My heart shattered—and then it rose. Because I knew exactly what that moment required.

I didn't question him. I didn't downplay it. I didn't ask if he was sure. I believed him. Fully. Immediately. Without condition. And maybe even more profoundly—I stayed calm. In a moment that could have sent me spiraling, when I wanted nothing more than to turn around and inflict the kind of harm that had been inflicted on him, I didn't react from rage. I centered my son. I focused on what he needed. And I gave it to him: safety, presence, and someone who chose action over avoidance.

That was the moment I realized the cycle had broken. The voice that had once been dismissed, doubted, or downplayed had become a refuge for someone else. All the times I had felt unheard—not necessarily disbelieved, but minimized, brushed aside, or left holding the weight alone—led me to this sacred moment. I showed up for my son in the exact way I had needed someone to show up for me. That choice—to trust him, to stay grounded, to protect without losing myself—wasn't just about parenting. It was about healing.

But the real shift—the monumental one—didn't happen all at once. It was the result of years of hardship and bad decisions, of relentless research, deep therapy, and a raw willingness to face my own reflection. It was the accumulation of trauma and the refusal to let it define me. It was reclaiming Utah—not by running from my past, but by walking straight into the heart of my community and making space for myself there.

It was choosing to be uncomfortable. To listen. To learn. To try again. It was desperation—the kind that comes from clawing your way out of the deepest hole and refusing to go back. It was pouring that desperation into something that mattered—filling my life with purpose until there was no room left for the old patterns that once kept me stuck. And more than anything, it was the fire I was born with. The stubbornness that refused to let the people who hurt me win. The knowing, deep in my bones, that I was meant for more than surviving. I was meant to be whole.

From that place, I began to show up as myself. And when I did, something beautiful happened: people saw me. Not the curated version. Not the girl who laughed through discomfort or minimized her pain. They saw the real me—raw, honest, unfiltered. And they didn't turn away. Some of them admired me. Some of them respected me. Some of them felt brave enough to tell their own stories.

I found love in the most unexpected places—in the brave vulnerability of strangers who shared their own stories after hearing mine, in the quiet solidarity of survivors who nodded from across a room, in the open arms of a community I built out of broken pieces. And in one person, in particular, I found something soft and steady. He saw me—not the cleaned-up version, but the messy, honest, still-healing me. His love wasn't frantic or conditional—it didn't demand a performance or a promise of perfection. It was peace instead of turbulence, consistency instead of chaos. And in that peace, I learned that love could be a safe place too.

Speaking up still isn't always easy. The fear of judgment, of personal attacks, of causing pain to loved ones, still lingers, a faint echo of past hurts. But I remain resolute. My voice—raw, imperfect, sometimes trembling, sometimes fierce—is my most precious gift, my most potent weapon against the silence that allows abuse and injustice to thrive. It is the key to my continued healing, to my wholeness.

I understand that not everyone possesses the same capacity or inclination to speak out as boldly as I now strive to. Trauma impacts us all differently, and sometimes silence is a necessary, valid strategy for survival. My intention in sharing my story, in finally using my voice without apology, is not to pressure anyone, but to offer hope, to illuminate a path. If you can use your voice, however small it may feel, do so. Let it be heard. And if you cannot, please know that you are not alone. There are people—myself included—working to create spaces where your story matters, your safety is prioritized, and your voice is never an inconvenience.

Find your community, whether it's through therapy, support groups, trusted friends, creative expression, or simply the quiet validation of another survivor's story. Get the story out, somehow, somewhere, even if only to yourself in a journal. Don't let the silence win.

Because in reclaiming my voice, I found my strength. In living my purpose, I found my peace. And in learning to love myself fully, I finally found my W.

Afterword

BY DOK WOODS, CMHC, LPC

THERAPIST, MENTAL PERFORMANCE CONSULTANT

It is rare to witness a story unfold that so gracefully holds both the ache of survival and the triumph of becoming. I have had the privilege of walking alongside Amber as she has journeyed through the deep, complex terrain of healing — not just for herself, but for her family, her community, and the generations to follow.

What began as a process of working through profound family trauma evolved into something extraordinary: a woman who reclaimed her voice, her identity, and her purpose. As a single mother of three remarkable sons, Amber has not only risen with fierce determination but has done so with tenderness, authenticity, and integrity. Her strength is not the kind that roars — it is the kind that steadies, that builds, that transforms.

Professionally, she has carved out space for herself in the demanding world of tech, where innovation often overshadows personal story. Yet, she brings both — intellect and soul — to every room she enters. And now, as an author, she gifts us the wisdom that only someone who has truly *lived* can offer.

This book is more than a testimony — it is a mirror, a guide, and an invitation. It will challenge you to sit with discomfort, to believe in resilience, and to remember that the past does not define the worth of one's future. Through these pages, you will meet a woman who chose to write a new narrative not only for herself, but for her children, and for all who seek healing.

To know Amber is to witness the embodiment of courage. To read her story is to believe again in the possibility of light after darkness.

May this book speak to the places in you that are still finding their voice — and may you find, as she has, that healing is not the end of the story, but the beginning of something beautiful.

Resources for Survivors

You are not alone. Whether you're just beginning your healing journey or have been walking this path for years, there is help, hope, and support available. The following resources have been personally meaningful to me and may be valuable to you as well.

Support & Healing Organizations

Saprea
Saprea is the nonprofit known for using proven, practical methods for confronting and overcoming child sexual abuse. Learn more about their free resources at www.saprea.org

RAINN (Rape, Abuse & Incest National Network)
The largest U.S. organization supporting survivors of sexual violence. Learn more at www.rainn.org

National Alliance on Mental Illness (NAMI)
Education, advocacy, and resources for those impacted by mental illness. Learn more at www.nami.org

Books That Helped Me Understand and Heal

- *The Body Keeps the Score* — Dr. Bessel van der Kolk
- *What Happened to You?* — Dr. Bruce Perry and Oprah Winfrey
- *No Bad Parts* — Dr. Richard C. Schwartz
- *Spilled Milk* — K.L. Randis
- *Codependent No More* — Melody Beattie

Understanding Trauma

If you're beginning to notice signs of trauma in your own story or the story of someone you love, know that this is a common experience — especially for survivors of childhood abuse. Trauma can impact the brain, body, and relationships in ways that are complex but completely valid. You deserve space to process, grieve, and rebuild — at your own pace, and in your own way.

Crisis Support

- Suicide & Crisis Lifeline (U.S.): Dial 988
- Text "HOME" to 741741 for 24/7 support from a trained crisis counselor
- Trevor Project (LGBTQ+ youth): www.thetrevorproject.org

Final Note from the Author

If you've made it this far, thank you. Truly.

This book is not just the story of my trauma — it's the story of what comes after. The story of finding my voice, reclaiming my worth, and refusing to carry shame that was never mine.

Whole Heals is the next chapter.

It is the place where I've poured everything I've learned — about trauma, healing, neurodivergence, motherhood, leadership, and voice — into something bigger than myself. A space for others to be seen, to be safe, and to be whole.

If you've resonated with my story, or if you're navigating one of your own, I hope you'll stay connected. There's more to come.

This may be the end of one book — but it's only the beginning. www.wholeheals.com

www.ingramcontent.com/pod-product-compliance
Lightning Source LLC
Chambersburg PA
CBHW060603150626
46553CB00024BA/1591